A TOAST TO SILENCE

A TOAST TO
SILENCE

Avoid Becoming Another Victim of Deceptive Police Tactics
By Knowing When and How to Use the Power of Silence

PETER BASKIN

New York

A TOAST TO SILENCE

Avoid Becoming Another Victim of Deceptive Police Tactics
By Knowing When and How to Use the Power of Silence

© 2016 PETER BASKIN.

Published in New York, New York, by Morgan James Publishing. Morgan James and The Entrepreneurial Publisher are trademarks of Morgan James, LLC.
www.MorganJamesPublishing.com

The Morgan James Speakers Group can bring authors to your live event. For more information or to book an event visit The Morgan James Speakers Group at
www.TheMorganJamesSpeakersGroup.com.

Shelfie

A **free** eBook edition is available
with the purchase of this print book.

CLEARLY PRINT YOUR NAME ABOVE IN UPPER CASE

Instructions to claim your free eBook edition:
1. Download the Shelfie app for Android or iOS
2. Write your name in **UPPER CASE** above
3. Use the Shelfie app to submit a photo
4. Download your eBook to any device

ISBN 978-1-63047-768-4 paperback
ISBN 978-1-63047-769-1 eBook
ISBN 978-1-63047-770-7 hardcover
Library of Congress Control Number:
2015914121

Cover Design by:
Chris Treccani
www.3dogdesign.net

Interior Design by:
Bonnie Bushman
The Whole Caboodle Graphic Design

In an effort to support local communities and raise awareness and funds, Morgan James Publishing donates a percentage of all book sales for the life of each book to Habitat for Humanity Peninsula and Greater Williamsburg.

Get involved today, visit
www.MorganJamesBuilds.com

Habitat
for Humanity
Peninsula and
Greater Williamsburg
Building Partner

TABLE OF CONTENTS

PREFACE

What's wrong with the following picture? It's 11 p.m. on Saturday and you and your spouse are driving home from a dinner party. You're talking about the impressive quality of the bouillabaisse, or maybe who insulted who as the evening progressed. As you talk, you see ahead of you flashing police lights. You wonder if there's an accident. The traffic slows to less than a crawl. Then it occurs to you why. It's a police checkpoint. They're looking for drunk drivers. You think, "Oh my God, I have had two—maybe three glasses of wine. What does that make my blood level? Will I be arrested?" And you think, "Damn, maybe I can make a U-turn and get out of it. But no, I see other officers. I shouldn't act suspicious. What do I do?"

In a few minutes, you're at the checkpoint. You roll down your window. The policeman in charge shines his flashlight in your face. He says "Good evening. May I see your license and registration?" You say, "Good evening, Officer, I'll get them." Then fumble through the glove compartment, and hand them to him. Trying to lighten the mood, you say, "Gee, it's pretty cold out there, your fingers must be freezing.", *or* something as lame. He looks at your identification.

He says, "Have you been drinking tonight, sir?"

You say, "I had a glass of wine."

He says, "One?"

You say, "I think so."

He shines a flashlight in your eyes, and then says, "Will you please step out of the car?"

You say, "OK."

He says, "I'd like you to take some tests for me."

You say, "Is that necessary?"

He says, "It's in your best interest. You can prove here and now that you're okay."

You say, "You fellows are doing a great job, I never want to be an impediment to law enforcement. I'll be happy to take any test you like."

So what's wrong with this? That you had two or three glasses of wine? No. That you didn't bolt, make a U-turn when you had the chance? No. That you lied about the number of glasses of wine you had? No. Let's play this picture again, the right way. You are driving home. You see the flashing lights. You realize it's a police checkpoint for alcohol. You don't know if you are over the legal limit. But that really doesn't matter, not tonight. You and your spouse arrive at the point where the officer asks you for your license and registration. He says. "Have you been drinking tonight, sir?" And you say to yourself, "I know what to do." A minute later, he lets you go. What exactly did you do? How did you beat the odds? That's what this book is about.

It's about knowing what to say and do at the most critical moment in the life of every case; the initial encounter with the police. This is when the success or failure of your case in court is largely determined. Most people don't know.

It's about making sure you are not counted among the twelve million people who are arrested annually in the U.S. following a police encounter, nine out of ten of whom are convicted because they were seduced by police lies into giving evidence by talking and taking tests, **before** the *Miranda* warning.

This book is a long overdue blue print to end the trashing of your Fifth and Sixth Amendment Constitutional rights by the police on the street, and to winning your case in court when accused of a crime. It is a detailed guide to recognizing police deception. The emphasis is on the day-to-day work done in America's criminal courts, which is out of the public eye. That day-to-day work overwhelmingly consists of traffic cases, misdemeanors, petty offenses, and alcohol and drug related misdemeanor offenses.

The focus is on the moment that the meeting between you and the officer begins. This is the critical time when your case is lost because you didn't know what to do, or not do, and what to say, or not say. This initial encounter is the beginning of the police gathering information and evidence against you. This moment should and can be the beginning of your successful defense. And what is the defense? It is not a Clarence Darrow summation by your lawyer in court. It is simply keeping your mouth shut, and not consenting to give evidence to the officer except giving your identity. Something that simple you are allowed to do.

I was hesitant, because of my regular contact and dealings with police officers in court, to use the words **lie** and **disinformation** to describe what most officers do during enforcement encounters with the public. But they are correctly used here. A lie is a deliberately false statement, something not true; disinformation is defined as information intended to mislead. Accordingly, **lie** is used throughout the text as the correct description of what police officers do when they confront you to obtain evidence with the definition of **disinformation** intended to be included.

There are countless books telling you what the law is, and hundreds written for lawyers. This book is not one of those. This book is written for folks who may need a lawyer, and will hopefully bring to the lawyer's office a winning case by using the law to work for them. Read on and end being deceived. The new approach I am urging is; don't talk to the police! I have never seen a case or situation where in the final analysis you're better off by choosing to talk to the police as opposed to not talking to them. Remaining silent is your right under the Constitution and this applies to the time **before officers arrest you**, that is, **before the *Miranda* warnings** are read or recited. That may not seem like a significant space of time but it is, and it is addressed at the heart of this book.

What I hope to accomplish in the pages that follow is to convince you that you can do this, in spite of a system, entertainment industry, and a popular culture, which has succeeded in having you believe you cannot or should not do this and to recognize what is really happening to you at the hands of the police, the government, showing you how to survive and win in the criminal justice system.

I detail for you the verbal and psychological tactics and methods used to deceive you or to trick you into believing you cannot, or should not, insist on and exercise your Fifth Amendment right not to be a witness against yourself. I point out both the direct as well as the less obvious ways the media, in all of its forms, conditions us to believe that you can't or shouldn't remain silent. I tell you how to exercise your rights which the police will try to convince you don't exist. You will learn the lies, deceptions, disinformation and misrepresentations the police use to manipulate you to talk, do yourself harm, and cause you to lose in court no matter who is representing you. When you open your mouth, you give evidence against yourself, and you lose. When you talk, take tests, and cooperate, in any of its forms on the street, your case is doomed from that point. It is only by luck or unusual fortuitous circumstance that a win might occasionally happen.

It is far better for you to learn to control and determine for yourself what happens in court. You do this by controlling and determining what evidence the police obtain from you.

It is simpler and easier that you think. At that first encounter with the police, you don't have the advantage of a lawyer's presence or advice. You're on your own. It's you, the Fifth Amendment, and the officer. Always remember, that at all times the Constitution places your importance above that of the government's agents—the police.

Police officers are not superhuman. They are ordinary men and women, with the power to arrest, nothing more. That's all they have, just the power to arrest, and a pass to lie to get evidence from you. They can't judge you, convict you, or punish you. Their opinion of your silence means nothing. Their conduct is always subject to review, and that review comes fairly soon when they do their job and bring you to the judicial officer immediately following an arrest. If you don't like what happens to you or your friends or family in court, you can fix it. The problem is not the law, not the system, not the police, not the judges, not your lawyer. It's you allowing the police to intimidate and/or con you into talking and cooperating.

In the pages that follow, I give you as comprehensive a set of scenarios, techniques, and verbal clues employed by the police that I'm able to recall from my experience with forty-eight years' worth of clients to alert you to what is happening, to protect your right not to give evidence against yourself, to make certain you do and say the right things to enable your lawyer to do his best for you and achieve a good result. That's why you pay a lawyer. That result is totally in your control, at the critical time of the beginning of a police encounter. When you don't talk, you win. It's as simple as that! To those who say, "Easier said than done.", keep reading.

While the emphasis in this book will be on the serious misdemeanor cases of driving while intoxicated and possession of marijuana, the advice given applies across the board to all criminal cases, whenever you meet the police on the street, or anywhere else.

The Fifth Amendment is not just words on paper, but useful and powerful ideas that are old and reliable friends, which will serve you well if you simply know them and exercise them correctly and at the right time and place. It reads:

> ### *"NO PERSON SHALL . . . BE COMPELLED IN ANY CRIMINAL CASE TO BE A WITNESS AGAINST HIMSELF."*

This book is not for the problem drinker, the alcoholic who still drinks, or the hard drug user. These folks probably won't follow any advice or exercise any judgment while actually intoxicated, or high. They do great damage, but they are fewer in number than is popularly believed. Not everyone who has had a drink or a hit of pot, is in a drunken stupor as is commonly thought. Activist groups have us believing that's true and apply direct pressure on judges to influence the outcome of Driving Under the Influence (DUI) cases.

They sit in court, usually up front, so the judges can't miss seeing them and they observe the trial, as is their right. If a defendant is acquitted, these folks often contact the press and name the judge involved.

This book is for the great majority of people from all walks and stations of life who may be convicted in court on too little evidence, most of which they unwittingly give up to the police unnecessarily, out of their own mouths, because they were victims of police deception.

I offer a different, counter-intuitive, and effective approach to handling the comprehensive catalog of police tactics and methods, which exploit the unjustified, but nearly universal fear of arrest. This fear needlessly causes you, during police encounters, to say and do all the wrong things, making mistakes that not only guarantee you getting arrested, but also causing you to lose your case in court. This new approach is summarized on a business card I developed and have been using for the past decade. Client feedback has been nearly one hundred percent positive. This approach outlined on the card in short form works. People who know and exercise their Fifth Amendment rights, which are quite simple, doing so at the right time and place and in the right way, win in court.

Readers will ask how a Virginia lawyer can speak for what is the law in every other state? The answer is found in the supremacy clause of the Constitution (Article Six) and Article Three Section Two which, read together, require that the Supreme Court's interpretation of the Bill of Rights must be followed in all fifty states, and to which ". . . the judges in every state . . ." are bound. The law everywhere is the absolute right to remain silent after you identify yourself.

Judges are starting to get the message. They are increasingly skeptical of the evidence traditionally provided by cops' observations repeatedly given with the usual training academy police lingo, which is regularly contradicted by police video recordings now increasingly used. The disparity between what the video shows and what the cop says it shows, is disturbingly wide and is being noticed. The camera doesn't lie, is not biased, nor does it have a stake in the outcome; as does a cop. The only other evidence judges usually hear is what you hand over voluntarily. If you stop talking, testing and cooperating, judges have less evidence to rule upon, evidence you can lawfully not give. When you remain silent, with passive, polite, non-belligerent, non-cooperation, you probably won't avoid arrest, but you will likely win where it matters, in court.

To those who suggest a connection between the recent upswing in police violence toward the people they encounter, and the exercise of their rights, I have two replies. First, there is no recent upswing; it is simply the same amount of police misconduct that has existed all along; just increasingly documented by cell phone video recording. Even though more newsworthy because we see them more, these violent, deadly encounters are still relatively small in number. The police are for the most part competent and do their job correctly notwithstanding my opinion of their methods when the total number of police stops and arrests is taken into account. We've seen a video of a police shooting about once every two months for the last year or so (2014-2015). The police have arrested thousands daily without incident, in the same period.

Second, we really have no choice but to insist upon and exercise our rights, especially the right to silence, because the alternative is intolerable, a police state based on fear of them and being afraid to speak up for and exercise our rights.

Conduct is the problem, not the right to silence. Running from the police, arguing with them, fighting with them, or resisting arrest is conduct, and doesn't work, as we have too frequently seen. Yet to be seen, however, is someone dying at the hands of the police after they said to an officer, "Sir, here is my ID. I have nothing else to say." and sticking to it.

The recent (2015) Sandra Bland arrest and death in a Texas jail and the Dubose shooting in Ohio, both following traffic infraction stops, illustrate the futility and danger of engaging in conversation with the police, even about the most trivial infractions. These two cases demonstrate how quickly and easily verbal engagement with the police leads to miscommunication, and misreading of intentions, escalating to disaster.

The police today are not the folks with whom to discuss or dispute anything on the street. To an officer, you are always wrong, thanks to the militarization of policing, resulting in officers thinking command structure, that you are subordinate to them, having a drill sergeant attitude, demeanor and inflexible ideas about what you are supposed to say and do in responding to their unfamiliar vocabulary. The result of your not complying exactly as they expect, repeatedly video recorded, is poor and ineffective communication with them, primarily caused by their domineering, condescending wording, tone, style, and short temper. You simply can't have a calm, civil, intelligent conversation with a drill sergeant. That's what they quickly become when you don't fit their expectation of being inferior to them.

Since communicating with them as an equal hasn't worked and has resulted in well documented tragedy, the best alternatives are minimal communication, consisting of immediately identifying yourself, then disengagement and silence. Our tradition of civilian control of police and the military will eventually turn on these drill sergeants and restore itself as they continue to be caught on camera mistreating and arresting folks without legitimate cause.

If we continue to do what we've been doing, fearing arrest, believing seductive police lies, talking and testing, nothing will change. Different, better results in court will come only from a different attitude and response when you meet the police. We don't have to do anything new. Simply do what has always been available, what works—silence. Given what's been happening as we have often seen of late, with those who run from, talk, argue, protest, or engage with them, silence and arrest could save your life as well.

PART 1
THE CULTURE OF DECEPTION

"(A) system of criminal law enforcement which comes to depend on the "confession" will, in the long run, be less reliable and more subject to abuses than a system relying on independent investigation."
—**Withrow v. Williams**, U.S. Supreme Court, 1993

"If the governed are misled, if they are not told the truth or if through . . . deception they lack information on which to base intelligent decisions, the system may go on— but not as a democracy."
—**David Wise**, *The Politics of Lying*

1

I began my legal career as a prosecutor in 1968 and a defense counsel since 1972. Throughout this time, I have observed in court, almost daily, what national statistics show year after year: Ninety percent of all criminal cases end by guilty pleas and convictions, primarily because the public doesn't know, and therefore doesn't exercise their most basic Constitutional right, to remain silent at the most critical moment in their case, the beginning of a police encounter.

There is a reason why, in the U.S.A., almost eleven million of the twelve million arrests annually end up in convictions on guilty pleas by those arrested and charged—unawareness caused by media fueled police **deception** about your right to remain silent and how, and especially when, to exercise it. The general public is shockingly deficient in its knowledge of this most basic right; what to say and do, **when** it matters most. Ten percent of these arrests (1.2 million in 2012) are for DUI and another 800,000 to 900,000 are for the possession of marijuana. How big is the target for the cops? Roughly 109.5 million people consume alcohol before getting behind the wheel, according to Mothers Against Drunk Driving (M.A.D.D.).

If M.A.D.D.'s numbers are correct, and there is no reason to doubt them, of those 109.5 million people only roughly one percent of that number get arrested annually for DUI. That's a lot of responsible people who drive without control problems, but to the cynic, a word which describes most cops well, that's 108.4 million drivers who don't get caught and are under the influence—highly doubtful. What I am addressing is those cases where the traffic stop is by an officer with a mindset, and because of things having little to do with safe driving; such as not using a turn signal, a tail light or a break light out, an air freshener hung from a rear view mirror, an expired tag. These things cause stops and start the ball rolling. Then deception from misinformation and fear of arrest leads to mistakes—talking, testing, and cooperating— and then you've been had, it's over, you lose.

This best known activist group (M.A.D.D.) has done admirable public service in bringing out the tragedies caused by irresponsible drinking drivers. These are the drivers who kill and maim. These drivers', statistics show, have a <u>B</u>lood <u>A</u>lcohol <u>C</u>ontent (BAC) averaging 0.16, which is twice the legal limit. The problem I address is not the efforts of M.A.D.D., but the legislative and judicial response when it comes to dealing with responsible drinking drivers who are often below the legal limit of 0.08 BAC when stopped, yet are assumed to be over the limit at the time of driving because that BAC is measured by a test administered approximately ninety minutes later. The result is the legislatures and the courts don't discriminate between doubtful and clear cases. My focus is on the doubtful, marginal cases, and how to avoid the government net that has become so wide and the mesh of the net so small that the system takes in and treats identically in terms of guilt or innocence (not punishment) those few who maim and kill with those, for example, who pull off the road to "sleep it off" in their vehicles. That's how absurd DUI enforcement has become and that's not the fault of M.A.D.D. It is legislative and judicial over-reaction which has only served to gather in large numbers of doubtful cases. These are the bulk of DUI cases that end up in convictions, and which keep the post-conviction bureaucracy well supplied with fee paying customers.

These borderline cases are the ones in which the police station breath/blood test is taken after the absorption clock has ticked to provide a false reading about the drivers' condition back at the time of the stop. The system created has thereby scooped up a lot of folks who are not drunk or under the influence when stopped, but are convicted nonetheless.

When I started practicing law in 1968, the threshold for DUI was 0.15. That number has come down in stages over the years to 0.12, then to 0.10, and now 0.08. Biology, toxicology and physiology have not changed in that short period of time. What has changed is politics and little else. It has been good politics to get tough on the drinking driver by convicting in many doubtful cases to assure catching and removing from the road the few truly dangerous drivers. This has an odd ring—our system is supposed to prefer letting go free one hundred guilty persons than convicting one who is innocent. It seems as though this notion is another of the many getting lip service only.

Deception comes from several sources, but overwhelmingly from the most influential driver of our popular culture about the police, the law, the courts, and the law enforcement method—the broadcast entertainment industry—television and movies. From these sources, our most basic individual rights are distorted, if not flatly misrepresented, and as a result, when the police are encountered, we are manipulated by them to do all the wrong things, causing damage which we, or the best, most experienced lawyers we may hire, cannot repair. This leaves little choice but to plead guilty. This should not, and does not, have to happen.

The number one reason why, upon encountering a police officer, we say and do all the wrong things, is the fear of being arrested by that officer, who is trained to stimulate that fear by deception. When we act on that fear with the very first words out of our mouths, our success in court is doomed, and before that, we still get arrested based on what we have said. There is no need for this fear. The entertainment and news industry contributes to that fear with its often inaccurate portrayal of the criminal law process, seemingly for the sole purposes of the dramatic effectiveness, financial success, and long running popularity of its widely watched police programming that infuses our popular culture with an inaccurate picture of the criminal law system. This results in a shortfall in our knowledge and a sense of futility which plays directly into the hands of the police, with disastrous consequences for your Constitutional rights on the street and your case in court.

> *"There is no refuge in confession but suicide . . . ."*
> —**Daniel Webster**

The police have two basic functions; community caretaking, and law enforcement. As community caretakers, modern police officers are on your side and are good, much appreciated public servants, honest, hardworking, and helpful. When it comes to law enforcement, the same cannot be said. In these instances, they are your opponent, and exhibit the exact opposite of honest, hardworking, and helpful. When stopped, you are isolated with your opponent, and you must be knowledgeable enough to keep yourself from being manipulated by their taking advantage of their authority figure status, appearance, manner, and tone, with seductive lies, often in the form of casual conversation, that masquerade as good police work. During police encounters, free speech is not free. It is very costly, and the less talking you do with the police, the far better off you will be, and you will be giving yourself the best chance of winning in court.

For its ninety percent conviction rate, at your expense, the criminal justice system depends on your confession or other damaging statements along with the test taking that are almost always made at the first contact with the police. Without these incriminating, self-destructive statements and test taking, that conviction rate would drop dramatically.

To take away the advantage the Bill of Rights gives you, the criminal justice system and our popular culture has conned you into relieving the government of its burden of proving guilt, transferring it, in most criminal cases to you by keeping you ignorant of your rights. This is possible because of inadequate education on this subject combined with entertainment industry and media practices.

The extent of the public's misconception of their most basic rights and when to use them, is astounding to the criminal law practitioner, and is not limited to just a relatively small criminal class nor just to ordinary folks, nor limited to just the major crimes dramatized on TV and on film. These basic rights apply in every criminal case, every offense. In the recent past, the rich and famous also have made the critical mistake of talking to the police or other government agents, and they all have one thing in common, they were convicted by and for what they said to these government agents, and not on the substantive crimes for which they were being investigated and eventually prosecuted, because they wouldn't shut up.

Exploiting you is a law enforcement community trained in, and armed with an array of verbal and psychological tactics to wear down any resistance to giving up your Constitutional right to remain silent. Every one of these tactics is based on lies, disinformation and deception. Their lies and deception are excused because of the perception reinforced by the entertainment and news industries portraying the police as the good guys, and the accused as the bad guys. So long as the police are bringing the bad guys to trial, the trickery done by the police to obtain evidence is the lesser evil, and therefore is okay. This is the dirty little secret on which our criminal justice system heavily depends.

In the virtual avalanche of police and prosecutor programming over the past twenty years, we see nonstop the verbal exchanges, "police speak", between the police and the accused. These verbal exchanges almost always begin with the misrepresentation about what will happen if you don't "cooperate" or "help" the police, and half-truths, distortions, and exaggerations about the trouble you're in, if not outright lies to heighten the fear of arrest and being jailed to get you to talk to them and say more than simply identifying yourself. Those lies cause you to do and say all the wrong things. Those lies and that fear are what the criminal justice system depends on to function smoothly and efficiently in order to process those twelve million cases as if the justice system was a case disposal assembly line.

Here is a list I have collected of some of the seductive lies, police speak, my clients have heard the past forty-eight years:

It will go easier for you if you talk.

You must answer my questions.

We just want to make sure you're okay to drive.

We want to hear your side.

This is your chance to tell your side.

Help us understand the situation.

You're not helping yourself by not talking to us.

You're being uncooperative.

Don't you want to cooperate?

We need to talk to you.

Talk to us now, or we'll take you in for questioning.

Don't you want to help us?

Don't you want to clear the air?

We need to find out what happened.

Do you want to go to jail?

Take responsibility for your actions.

The tests can prove your innocence.

You need to perform some tests for us.

If you don't answer, you're obstructing justice.

If you don't have anything to hide, you would talk to us.

If you don't have anything to hide, you would let us search.

You don't need a lawyer if you didn't do anything wrong.

I will tell the prosecutor you cooperated.

I will tell the judge you cooperated.

We're offering you the opportunity to take some tests.

If you're sober you can pass these tests.

I'm going to have you do some test to see if you're alright.

That's not how the system works (if you chose to remain silent and not test).

The judge will appreciate your honesty with me.

This breath test device will help us determine if you're okay.

Who's going to take care of your kids if I take you to jail?

Give us the information we want or we'll arrest you for obstruction of justice.

You have only one thing going for you and that's the ability to cooperate.

We can't help you until you help us.

You don't want to talk? Okay, be a smartass.

What's your lawyer going to tell you that you don't already know?

Be honest with us.

These lies and misrepresentations about you and your rights don't get thrown at you by accident. This is the number one method of law enforcement that police officers are trained to deliberately use to get you to give up your most potent defense tools, the right to silence, and legal counsel at the most critical moment. They induce you to fear exercising your rights by telling you inaccurately what will happen if you don't "cooperate". Then, when out of that fear you cooperate, police speak for giving up your Constitutional rights to silence and counsel, run your mouth and take tests, the police do exactly what you were afraid of, and what you feared. They arrest you based on your cooperation, your words, and most importantly, you lose in court. This is, purely and simply, exploitation of deception at its worst. A Great American Con Job.

What we were all taught in social studies when we were school children now has real life context. Your Constitutional rights are few in number, and simple to learn and implement. If you are smart enough to learn how to use a smart phone, you can learn when to shut up. You can also learn the most effective way to exercise those rights, clearly and with calm firmness, so that there is no misunderstanding by the officer as to what you are doing and saying, as well as what you are not doing and not saying.

The officer has the power to be very disagreeable. He can arrest you, but that's about it. He's done after that. The fear of arrest is misplaced because in our current criminal law system, arrest is of comparatively very short duration in the overwhelming majority of cases. Not only are misdemeanors and traffic arrests of short duration, arrests matter little if you win in court. What should be feared is getting convicted, which probably won't happen if you simply shut up. It is getting convicted which has all of the nasty consequences, which are long lasting, costly, and very burdensome.

Getting convicted is the fear to have. Exercising the right to silence at the right time and place and in the correct manner is the best way to avoid conviction. If you must be afraid of something when you are stopped by a police officer, be afraid of conviction, which the Constitution gives you the power to avoid, not of arrest. Just as in personal health, in criminal law prevention is the best medicine. All of the tactics, ploys, and deceptions used by the police to get you to serve up a case against yourself, fall flat when you, knowing you can be silent, do exactly that with a small number of exceptions which are as easy to learn as your basic right to silence.

As often as not, the police don't know what to do with someone who effectively exercises their right to silence, except to play their one trump card, which is to arrest you. After that occurs, they are done, and your trump card, silence, takes over. Your silence on the street is that prevention where it counts, in court. Silence on the street rarely loses in court!

The lies, misrepresentations, and deceptive images utilized by the police are many and varied. They are as limitless as the officer's imagination and the breadth of the English language. Police speak has a few common, easily recognizable themes, however. Those themes are identified so that no matter what the educational level of the officer, or his skill with the English language, you will recognize his purpose, and that flashing strobe light will go on in your head telling you the right things to say and do; **nothing!**

Deceptive police and media created images include an expectation of being required to submit to being interrogated by the police, the expectation that the police will get you to confess, that "lawyering up," as guaranteed by the Sixth Amendment before interrogation, is wrong and the big problem, that you are required to give roadside answers and explanations, take roadside sobriety tests, consent to searches, or do anything more than identify yourself. If you don't "cooperate," which is police speak for talking, testing and giving up your rights, you are breaking the law, obstructing justice, and going to jail.

All of these police and media created images are false. To the extent these images are real, it's only because we have let them exist by default. Why and how this has happened, as well as how this can be fixed are questions having simple, direct answers that are the purpose and focus of "A Toast to Silence". Read, remember and be deceived no more.

Most people don't regard themselves as criminals and many people in a lifetime never encounter a member of law enforcement, except perhaps to ask directions, or when donating to the Fraternal Order of Police. The days of the foot patrolman walking the neighborhood and chatting with the residents are long gone, and most of us regard ourselves as law abiding citizens. Why then, would we need this book? The answer is the number of people who haven't a clue is shocking, when it comes to their most basic rights. You may have vague ideas, but don't know how, or **when** put them to work. You don't realize how the police con you into talking—the unrecognized verbal seduction and manipulation the police utilize the very first moment they meet you, causing you to self-destruct.

If you drive a car, have children of driving age who use the family car, take their friends into your car or home while you're away from home, or on vacation, go to parks, school activities, sporting events, rock concerts, places where alcohol or marijuana are consumed, attend happy hour after work, have a drink or two, and then head home, go out to a sports bar to watch a game, have your college age kids throw a noisy party at your apartment, condo, or single family home, you will most probably encounter the police. This list is not exhaustive, but you get the idea. Police go to these places because they are dispatched there to find people who may be breaking the law. Some people in these everyday life situations may be breaking the law, some don't know if they are. All have a right to a reasonable expectation of privacy from government intrusion and the right to remain silent, not be compelled to give testimonial evidence against themselves, and the right to not abdicate these rights by reason of unawareness of them. My objective is to help you to become aware of your rights, commit them to memory, and to recognize the situations and verbal clues from the police, where the potential for creating legal problems for yourself arise. These problems can be avoided and prevented, or at least minimized by knowledge of and exercising these basic rights, so that when the police approach you, the first thing that you'll think is: I will remain silent, and demand a lawyer before being questioned, and not answer any question except about my identity.

Sooner or later, most people will experience an encounter with the police, or other law enforcement personnel—a county or city police officer, a deputy sheriff, a state trooper, or highway patrolman. What you do and say during these first moments, and little else, will determine the outcome of your case in court.

As a criminal defense lawyer, my only objective is to obtain the best result for my client in court. During my nearly half century career as prosecutor and defense counsel, I have learned that the only way I can do my best for my client is for them to lay the best possible groundwork for their defense. That groundwork is for my client or any potential client, to know what to do and what to say if stopped. More important, it is knowing what not to do and not to say and it is really quite simple. It is not magical, mysterious, or complicated. It is basic knowledge taught to all of us, relatively early in life. You don't need to have gone to law school.

When the Fifth Amendment was added to the Constitution in 1789 most people had very little schooling, and today we learn about it, perhaps in middle school, certainly by high school. When taught however, the Fifth Amendment regrettably is passed over quickly, touched upon superficially, and then misunderstood, criticized, misstated, maligned, and lied about.

The Fifth Amendment right to silence is the right least remembered when a person first meets the officer, the right least honored by the police, and most resisted by them during these encounters. Yet, it is the most potent weapon of self-preservation in our legal system that an individual has when confronted, because not talking keeps from them the strongest evidence there is against you.

Police encounters, detentions, and arrests have one purpose; to detect crime and prosecute the persons accused. I'm not talking primarily about the serious crimes of murder, rape, robbery, kidnapping, although my approach works for them as well. I'm talking about the petty offenses committed by ordinary people that form the bulk of our courts' business, and is the day-to-day work of the criminal law practitioner; traffic offenses, petty misdemeanors, possession of marijuana, alcohol related offenses; the types of crimes committed by those who would not likely regard themselves as criminals. Twenty-five million Americans smoke pot, and at least four times that number drink alcohol to some degree and do so before getting behind the wheel.

From the most serious crime to the most petty, the law enforcement system depends on evidence from the accused, and when they leave the courthouse many are embittered with feelings that they were not treated fairly because of the absence of any other independently obtained evidence.

It is no surprise, that the people are unhappy with the work product of that system which is comprised of judges, prosecutors, police, lawyers, rules of law, rules of evidence and a post-conviction bureaucracy. What comes as a surprise is where and why they place the blame for their unhappiness. The last thing they want to hear, and the most difficult thing for a lawyer to tell his client is that they are at fault because they opened their mouths.

These folks, unhappy with the system, wouldn't keep quiet, because they didn't know when they could. Against them and their unawareness of the timing of their right to remain silent, their right not to consent to any search, their right to say no to sobriety test requests, or demands, their right not to have to admit or explain anything, is a police officer who is specifically trained to talk them out of, and to give up those rights. The officers' arsenal of ploys, manipulation, and lies, particularly the misstatement of the law, and stimulating a fear of arrest to get you to talk and supply evidence against yourself, is nothing short of astounding and is limited only by the officer's imagination, your perceived vulnerability to giving in, to giving up your rights, the unjustified fear of arrest, and you mistakenly thinking your right to silence begins with the recital of the *Miranda* warning at the moment of arrest.

The officers' formidable arsenal is useless, however, when you know your rights, and exercise those rights. All that needs to be done by you is to remember to say right up front;

"I choose to remain silent", "I demand to speak with a lawyer before speaking to you", and "I have nothing else to say".

A large contributor to deception is semantic fraud. Starting with the use and misuse of the word "justice", it is the popular understanding of the word that is the problem. We all hear from time to time the phrase "bring someone to justice", signaling to us the word is intended to be limited to punishing the wrongdoer, who, from the outset is viewed as guilty, thanks to pre-trial publicity. To the lawyer who understands the system, and his role in it, justice is as much, if not more, about the process; how we get from accusation to punishment. To the criminal defense lawyer, justice is done regardless of the outcome of the trial if the process is fair by observance of all of the rights of the accused, not just when he arrives at the courthouse for his trial, but also from the beginning of the process. If all the rules are followed from the first moment of a police encounter, all the constitutional protections observed, and the procedures and rules of a fair trial followed, the process and the outcome, whether guilty or not guilty, is justice. Unless all of this happens, justice has not been done.

The justice process begins with the initial collection of evidence to be used at trial. This collection process in most misdemeanor cases begins with the police stopping you. That collection process has rules to go by. Those rules have their roots and continued vitality in the Bill of Rights. If those rules are not followed by the government, and insisted upon by defense lawyers, justice can never happen, no matter how much window dressing is supplied by the remainder of the process.

Often when you are stopped, and appear nervous, the officer will try to calm down the tension with reassuring statements such as "We just want to find out what happened", "We need to hear your side", "This is your chance to tell us your side" (suggesting only one such chance, right then and there), or "If you have nothing to hide, you will talk to us". Don't be fooled by such statements. These statements and others of this kind illustrate law enforcement's skill at lying as officers routinely do to obtain evidence, without actually appearing to lie. Such invitations to tell your side to the officer also illustrate the police's and the public's unawareness of basic principles of due process as applied to the criminal law. Due process is another basic right you are guaranteed in the Fifth Amendment.

If you ask most people what due process means, they answer that it has something to do with fairness and opportunity to hear both sides of a dispute. That's fine and is a workable layman's definition, but if you ask most people how it works in a criminal proceeding, they either don't know, or think due process means both sides should be heard, or must be heard. **Wrong! Big mistake!**

In all criminal cases, from minor traffic offenses to capital murder, due process means the state (or other accusing body) has the burden of proof. It must prove your guilt beyond a reasonable doubt, as to each and every element of the offense charged. That burden to produce evidence and prove the case never shifts to you. You are presumed innocent. This presumption of innocence alone, is sufficient to find you "not guilty" unless that burden of the government is met. You are never required to produce evidence, or a defense, unless and until the government has met its burden of proof and even then, there's no requirement that you prove anything or provide any evidence. Even if you are guilty as sin, due process means you have the right to insist that the government prove it without the help of what comes out of your mouth. You can be guilty as sin and not be lying when you plead not guilty. Such a plea merely announces you're exercising the constitutional due process right to require your accuser to prove your guilt. Pleading not guilty is not a statement of fact; it is the procedural mechanism by which a criminal trial begins.

When you choose not to testify or talk to the police, I use the word "election". Regrettably, most judges, prosecutors, police and the media refer to such elections, or choices, as "failure" or "refusal". The defendant failed to answer questions, failed or refused to testify, failed or refused to cooperate. This is wrong, and to some extent, is the fault of the criminal defense bar. I, and a few, too few, of my colleagues, make it a point to correct in court any prosecutor, police officer, or judge who describes the exercise of a Constitutional right or a due process right as a failing or a refusal. The media, even more so, is doing great public disservice with such wording since they have a wider audience than the criminal defense bar. Choosing or electing to exercise a constitutional right is not a refusal or a failure, it is an intelligent choice. Leading Constitutional Law Scholar, Harvard Law School Professor Lawrence H. Tribe, in his second edition, <u>American Constitutional Law</u> said it this way:

> So long as an individual's answer to official questions might be employed by the questioning jurisdiction as evidence, or leads to evidence, in a future criminal prosecution of that individual, the Fifth Amendment applicable to the states through the Fourteenth Amendment confers a **privilege** to be silent. Exercise of such a **privilege** can neither be equated with guilt, nor treated as a forbidden **failure** to cooperate with a proper inquiry and used by the government as the basis for adverse treatment.

Perhaps the greatest semantic fraud is the word "cooperate". When you are stopped by the police, cooperation has two versions; theirs and yours. Their version means you give them evidence against yourself by answering questions, making admissions and taking tests. Yours is to be calm, civil and respectful in word, tone, and manner, including conduct which assures them that you are not a danger to their safety, but giving no verbal or test evidence. The problem with the term "cooperating" in the context of law enforcement is that cooperating suggests teamwork. Teamwork is intended to be engaged in by teammates. The police are not, never will be, and never have been your teammate. They and the government are your opponents. As long as there remains no legal requirement to cooperate, once you are in the adversarial process that is our legal system, which begins at the initial police encounter, **don't do their version. Do yours**. Not cooperating does not make matters worse for you, only for your opponent, the government. Remaining silent makes matters better for you and your lawyer. If you waive your rights (cooperate), no lawyer can save you except by begging for a break from the prosecutor. You don't have to beg when the prosecution has a weak case, and a weak government case is, in my experience, weak when there are no statements or test results from your cooperation to use against you.

That doesn't mean that you are not a good person and you should not consider yourself a bad person if you don't cooperate as they view it. Always remember that if the police had the evidence, independent of what you tell them, they would have no need to talk to you, or obtain your cooperation. Their questioning of you is always done for the purpose of using what you tell them against you to prove your guilt, or to fill out and strengthen a weak and incomplete case against you. Their questioning of you is their signal to you, their confession to you, that they can't successfully prove a case against you in court without your statements, admissions, explanations, or taking of tests. Unless you want to be convicted of the offense with which you are charged, don't talk and don't test. If you do otherwise, you will lose.

PART II
THE GREAT AMERICAN CON JOB

> *"I became a policeman because I wanted to be in a business where the customer is always wrong."*
> —Unnamed Officer quoted by Arlene Heath
>
> *"I have never seen a situation so dismal that a policeman couldn't make it worse."*
> **—Brendan Behan**

n 1964, United States Supreme Court Justice Arthur Goldberg observed and wrote in his opinion in the case of ***Escobedo v. Illinois***:

No system of criminal justice can or should survive if it comes to depend for its continued effectiveness on the citizens' abdication through unawareness of their Constitutional Rights.

No system worth preserving should . . . fear that if an accused is permitted to consult with a lawyer, he will become aware of and exercise these rights.

With those words the Court was saying not only what should be, it was describing the American criminal justice system in the real world as it actually is now and was in 1964. The prosecution of criminal cases does, in fact, depend on the unawareness of the accused of their rights in order for the system to function to its advantage.

The criminal justice system relies on the confession and guilty plea of the accused in ninety percent of criminal cases. Without incriminating statements out of the mouth of the accused, the system could grind to a halt and be suffocated and overwhelmed by trials in which other forms of proof would be required, but often lacking, absent the statements of the accused.

The confession yields guilty pleas, also known as plea bargains, or deals in well over ninety percent of all criminal cases, from the most minor to the most serious. How does this happen? Why does this happen? It happens because society has managed to transfer the governments' burden of proving guilt in criminal cases to the accused, by keeping the accused ignorant of their Constitutional rights, and manipulating them to talk and take tests.

This is relevant to your life more than you realize. It is not limited to just a relatively small so called criminal class, nor ordinary folks, nor just the poorly educated. Northern Virginia, where I practice primarily is very affluent with well-educated people. Over half of the population here, from which juries and clients are drawn, hold four year college and postgraduate degrees. The D.C. metro area has over six million people. That's a lot of smart people, yet my colleagues and I have no shortage of clients, and there is plenty of legal business in criminal cases. Northern Virginia conducts about one-third of all legal business in the entire state.

The rich and famous have also made the mistake of talking to the police or other government agents. Martha Stewart, Scooter Libby, baseball's Barry Bonds and Roger Clemens all have one thing in common: they talked to the police and were prosecuted with what they said. Interestingly enough, the substantive offenses with which they were charged, went nowhere. They were all found guilty of giving false statements to investigators and little else. In Roger Clemens' first trial, he was saved by luck, a mistake prosecutors rarely make. Not anything he or his lawyer did. Certainly not by keeping his mouth shut at the beginning. That's pretty thin ice on which to skate. Relying on your opponent's mistakes may work well in sports, but not so well in the criminal law.

Why did they open their mouths? They didn't have to. If they were advised by counsel to explain themselves, they were very poorly advised. When it comes to the Fifth Amendment, the media is to blame, to a large extent because instead of policing the government, as originally intended by the First Amendment, the media has become the government's helper and promotes the notion that invoking the Fifth Amendment is self-incrimination, an admission of guilt instead of the constitutional right not to do so. The word self-incrimination does not appear in the Fifth Amendment. Its origin is unclear to me, but it is the darling word of the media. Instead of reporting that someone chose to be silent, they report "He refused to incriminate himself." The legal profession shares the blame by both not publicizing and not counseling the use of the Fifth Amendment, and the propriety of seeking its protection.

The correct way to phrase "taking the Fifth" is to incorporate its central idea, compelled speaking. Any short, concise combination of words mentioning this element or referring to this part of the Fifth Amendment is sufficient. Keep it simple, "I choose to remain silent", or "I have nothing to say." Any other phrasing, and especially the use of that media favorite, self-incrimination sounds awkward, and immediately causes the listener to think the person invoking their Fifth Amendment privilege is guilty of something because of the incriminating content of the answer not made to the question. Thus, the exact opposite effect occurs of what was intended in 1789 by the authors of the Fifth Amendment. The listener thinks the person remaining silent looks guilty, as many clients have said to me over the years.

The current state of the playing field on which encounters with the police take place is a disaster waiting to happen for the Fifth Amendment. Not only has it not been emphasized to us early, it is disparaged and belittled, when not ignored outright, in the news and entertainment media, incorrectly verbalized when invoked, and those invoking it are viewed negatively at best, or guilty at worst. If that weren't enough, the law enforcement community is trained and armed with an array of verbal and psychological tactics, using deception, misinformation and seductive lies to wear down any resistance to giving up your privilege to remain silent. Virtually every such verbal and psychological device the police use as detailed in these pages is based on lies told to you by the good guys. This is the message being sent. The other media created message is that of an expectation of you being required to submit to interrogation and the expectation of confession; the police will get you to confess.

I'm not a celebrity lawyer and I've never represented a celebrity. I've been a working criminal defense lawyer, representing ordinary people. I've had a fair share of locally newsworthy cases, (the murder of a police officer during a bank robbery and the murder of a businesswoman by her employee to name two), and have defended cases ranging from parking tickets to capital murder and just about everything in between. My daily work in the criminal courts of Virginia has involved a wide cross section of people, educated and not as educated, professionals, military personnel, blue and white collar people, young and old, men and women, teachers, students and housewives. They all have had two things in common. They are shockingly unaware of their Fifth Amendment rights and that unawareness has resulted in their being found guilty in court because they didn't, to put it bluntly, shut up. Why? Because they didn't realize they could, nor when and how they should, and especially **when** they should **not** speak.

How can this be fixed? By education, beginning with the first exposure to social studies and continuing with energetic publicity and advocacy by criminal defense lawyers. And also by understanding that what you see on TV and in the movies and what you read from courtroom news reports are not accurate reflections of basic rights. All such programs and films should begin with a warning disclaiming the legal accuracy of their legal content.

I came to realize this at about the turn of the millennium. I came home one evening, greeted my wife, who was watching a law and order TV show, and I said to her "I would sit down and watch with you but I don't want to watch the TV version of what I see every day in court."

As I was pouring us a drink, I overheard something on the show and it startled me into commenting, "Damn, no wonder folks say and do all the wrong things to the police."

I then asked her how often she watched these shows and she replied, "Regularly. They're entertaining." I decided to sit down and watch regularly with her, and after a time it dawned on me. Folks who watch this stuff are badly misled. No wonder the guilty plea and conviction rate is what it is. Every episode had several things wrong or inaccurate about our rights when confronted by the police. The cause and effect connection was clear.

The most popular cop show in television history is Law & Order, which in the original version ran for twenty seasons on NBC, and still is a force in reruns and spinoffs. It was well written, acted and produced. But it has also misled. If you've watched it, you'll know the following scene:

Two veteran detectives corral a suspect while he is loading a truck with whatever it is he delivers. The suspect continues loading while he's questioned (as if visits by cops are everyday occasions), and gives perfunctory and evasive answers. One of the detectives says, "It'll go best for you if you cooperate", "Maybe we ought to do this down at the station", or "If you know what's good for you, you'll tell us what we want to know." These suspects almost always give in. They seem to have no choice. But, in real life, they do. It's just that nobody seems to know this.

I entered law school in 1964. In that year, the Supreme Court decided what I consider to be one of the most important and significant opinions on the Constitutional rights of the accused. Even though it is regarded as dealing with the Sixth Amendment right to counsel before trial, and has received less publicity that the famous case of ***Miranda v. Arizona*** decided two years later, it is, in my view, equally important because it paved the way for *Miranda.* That case is *Escobedo v. Illinois.* In these two opinions, the Supreme Court interpreted the constitution to mean that all persons accused of a crime, whether it be a misdemeanor, a DUI charge, or a felony, first have the right to silence, when first placed under arrest and second, to have counsel present and specifically tell the person arrested of his right to remain silent and not be a witness against himself, not to say anything and to remain silent **before** being questioned.

Why don't people take advantage of these rights? I have interviewed hundreds of accused clients and I always ask, regardless of the charge, the same two questions: What did you say, or rather, what are the police going to say you said to them when questioned? When the client, with rare exception, tells me what he or she said to the questioning officer, usually something very damaging to their case, I tell them what they told the police will result in losing their case. I then ask: Why did you say that, why did you answer the officer?

The client then typically answers:

I didn't know I didn't have to answer.

I thought I had to answer.

I didn't know I could remain silent.

I thought it would be easier for me to cooperate with the officer.

I thought he wouldn't arrest me.

I didn't know I didn't have to consent to the officers' request to search me or my car or my home without a search warrant.

I didn't know I could decline to submit to those breath and field sobriety tests (if stopped while driving).

I didn't know I could insist on having a lawyer present when questioned.

I didn't want to lie to the officer.

The officer didn't advise me of my *Miranda* rights.

I answered because I didn't want him to think I was guilty.

I was afraid.

I was intimidated.

I thought I could only remain silent after he told me I could.

I didn't know.

How do we continue to forget something so basic and so valuable as the right to remain silent? An hour or two on this part of the Fifth Amendment out of an entire semester of Constitutional law in law school is, in my view, wholly inadequate teaching on this vital subject. It is simply not taught to our young, nor stressed by our lawyers as it should be, and hardly ever mentioned in news reports.

When it comes to the Fifth Amendment, our schools, particularly high schools, contribute to this shortfall by employing a practice which in my view is especially insidious. It is the current practice of placing police officers in the schools. These officers, which are politely referred to as "school", or "community resource" officers, are utilized in a way which is little more than subversive, under the guise of teaching students respect for authority. The problem is not police officers being present in the schools. It is rather, how they are used by school authorities.

When a student is suspected of, or reported to have been involved in questionable or illegal activity, he is summoned to the principal's office for questioning, often without being told why. How fair is that? He is then questioned by the principal without the protection of *Miranda* because he is not under arrest. This questioning is conducted by the principal in the presence of the community resource officer, the police, who then prosecutes the student after he makes damaging statements or admissions in a so-called showing of "respect for authority".

The Fifth Amendment protects persons. It is not limited to citizens. There is no age, circumstance, race, nationality, or gender exception. Students are persons, yet this so-called respect for authority lesson comes at the expense of the more important civics lesson, the Fifth Amendment. Great teaching! Schools should be proud of themselves for their contributions to ignorance in placing governing authority over the importance of individual rights. They might as well be saying openly "screw the Constitution".

Compounding the shameful shortfall in our education is the damage done by television. During my career, I've watched how TV coverage of nationally publicized criminal cases has misshaped the public's view of criminal law. After first reporting the crime and the arrest, they then discuss the evidence against the accused as provided by one side only, the police. Next they describe how the police interrogation of the accused is progressing, leaving the impression that police interrogation is inevitable, expected, and required. It is neither mandatory nor inevitable. No one has to submit to questioning whether on the street, in custody, or at any time, particularly in the interval between the initial contact with the officer and being arrested.

Then as the case progresses, the media interviews nationally famous lawyers who comment on the impact upon the trial jury of damaging admissions the accused has made to the police. With one exception in my memory, Gerry Spence, commenting during the O.J. Simpson case, all these nationally known lawyers ought to quit criminal practice or are guilty of malpractice for not saying publicly when interviewed, that the accused should have been advised to remain silent and should have not submitted to police questioning to begin with.

If, as *Miranda* and the Fifth Amendment state, the accused has the right to remain silent, why doesn't it happen? It doesn't happen for these reasons: Failed education at all levels, timid lawyers, police lies, deception and manipulation, and finally, media conditioning, with more and seemingly nonstop deception and misinformation about when the right to silence begins.

Considering first, timid lawyers, as portrayed by the entertainment industry, they virtually ignore the Fifth Amendment. These TV shows all begin the same way and progress the same way. The show by the actual name "Law & Order" wastes no time in misrepresenting the real world. The very first words we hear, announcing the start of that program, are a lie. "The people are represented by two equally important groups, the police and the prosecutor . . .". The police represent the people? Really? **Nonsense!** The police don't represent the people. They represent the government. They exploit the people with disinformation and with lots of help from the media, by misinforming you about your right to remain silent. Then in the opening scenes, the crime is discovered, a suspect is developed, and then arrested. As the arrest is announced, the handcuffs are put on the accused, and the *Miranda* warnings begin, the very first line of which is the Fifth Amendment right to remain silent. Then, at the critical moment of the *Miranda* warning recital, the scene and the audio fade to a commercial and we don't hear the critical feature of the warning. What we hear last is "you have the right to a lawyer". What we don't hear is the remainder of the sentence, the right to a lawyer "before and during questioning". This is the critical moment in, and the groundbreaking feature of the *Miranda* decision. It is at that moment, when questioning then begins, that the accused does the most damage to his case if unrepresented by competent counsel, if he hasn't already made damaging pre-arrest, pre-*Miranda* statements. This leaves the very wrong impression that the right to a lawyer and to remain silent occurs only **after** arrest and you talk to the police. Dead wrong. I recognize that the dramatic success of these shows depends on the "breaking" of the accused by interrogation and getting him to confess. I also recognize and submit that this dependence on dramatic success badly misleads the public in a significant way. My clients over the years have convinced me that they believe they must submit to interrogation. The right to remain silent means the exact opposite. No person must submit at any time or place, to police interrogation whether under arrest or not, whether given the *Miranda* warning or not, no matter what the charge, no matter when.

If the fade away to a commercial at the critical moment of these programs, when the accused needs counsel the most, is damaging to the public's perception of what their rights are when questioned at the initial encounter, that beat goes on during the next segment of these programs. In these segments, we see the accused questioned in what has seemingly become the required process the accused must endure, police questioning, to the point of breaking, giving in, and confessing.

Nothing in the law requires this to occur. The accused need only announce that he intends to remain silent and demand to have a lawyer present. The questioning then **must** stop immediately. The police must await the presence of the lawyer before resuming questioning, if the lawyer who appears is dumb enough to allow that to happen, before getting something for his client in return.

When the accused occasionally announces that he demands a lawyer, we are then exposed to the disdainful facial expressions of displeasure and annoyance by the police at the accused lawyering up. Not only the facial expressions, but the tone and inflection in the voice tells us that lawyering up is somehow a bad thing, a disappointing thing, an antisocial thing, an uncooperative thing, the wrong thing to do. The detectives and prosecutors on these shows, when they react to the accused's assertion of his constitutional rights in this manner, are telling the viewing public that invoking the right to silence and to counsel is wrong. All I can say is, "Hey, media idiots, lawyering up is everyone's basic right, remember?" Maybe when your teacher covered the Bill of Rights you fell asleep after the part about freedom of speech. If you really think lawyering up and remaining silent are bad ideas, why don't you have the brass to openly advocate repeal of the Fifth and Sixth Amendment? Have the backbone to say directly what you imply indirectly, or include in lawyering up, that it is a constitutional right as is remaining silent, or just shut up on this subject or any other aspect of the law you constantly demonstrate you know little about.

As the program continues, we're treated to an occasional episode where the lawyer for the accused shows up in the interrogation room. When that happens, we see a shamefully incompetent fool who sits silently next to his client while he is questioned, again for dramatic effectiveness. The client gives all the damaging answers the police want or need and it is then, at this point, the lawyer comes to life, opens his mouth and tells the client stop talking. Too late! The lawyer should have done that first thing upon entering the interview room, and meeting his client. The lawyer should have directed the client to say nothing and then announce to the police the interview was not happening and demand that his client be returned to his cell, instructing him to remain silent. After two decades of these weekly shows, and reruns 24/7, it is no surprise that the public expects interrogation by the police which is portrayed as required, cannot be resisted, and that demanding legal counsel is futile. The message these programs deliver is: the police will break your resistance, a lawyer is useless, you must submit to questioning and you will confess. The climate has been thus created of an expectation of confession, an expectation of you having no real rights you can rely on, and an expectation of the government always winning. Fully half of the running time of the show is almost always devoted to the interrogation of and confession by the suspect, often accompanied by his or her lawyer, who is portrayed as brain-dead because that's how the script is written for him or her; the defendant's lawyer does nothing until it's too late, and the client has confessed. I can't recall a single episode in which a suspect arrested with or without the advice of counsel remained silent, and the prosecution proved its case against the suspect. Only when the suspect talks does the prosecution win. The lesson that should be learned from these programs—remain silent and you win!

It is mainly TV which has enabled the police to deceive and trick you into saying and doing the wrong things on the street. Law & Order TV programming has evolved from its initial portrayal of law enforcement personnel as clever, sarcastic, wisecracking, often bullying authority figures always getting the confession. Currently, a number of TV law enforcement people are portrayed as super intuitive high tech geeks who analyze the psychology of their targets, narrating for the viewer how everyone thinks and then, like the skilled chess player, anticipate the suspects' next move and intercept them in the nick of time, telling us that the police are smarter than anyone and fooling many.

The police are not smarter than anyone else. They simply take advantage of the culture of deception which TV has for years conditioned us into accepting as reality what is shown when it comes to talking to, being questioned by, answering, and cooperating with the police. All of their TV cleverness, psychological insight and computer savvy go nowhere until someone talks, as they still need you to talk and engage with them. They still depend on your opening your mouth. They now have added to their arsenal that they can read your mind, so you might as well cooperate and confirm for them what they lead you to believe they already know or can prove.

This form of deception is pure crap, but seemingly never lets up because it sells. As a result, the guilty plea rate does not go down from a steady ninety percent for two reasons only; you can't or won't say no to talking and cooperating with the police.

The media is supposed to be the voice of truth in response to government deception. The media is supposed to police the police. When it comes to the Fifth Amendment and your other basic rights during your encounter with the police, the truth about your rights is the last thing you hear, if you hear it at all, from either the police or the media's portrayal of the police.

The excuse usually given for this betrayal of the public is that TV and movies provide entertainment, not reality, and we are supposed to recognize the difference. This "entertainment" has conditioned us not to recognize the difference and we pay dearly when we meet the police. There is just enough authenticity and accuracy in the television portrayal of how the police and the criminal justice system work to give the impression that what is shown is for the most part true and accurate. The reality is, there is not much accuracy, if there is any mention at all of your rights. There is almost zero push back against the distortion of the truth about these basic rights, especially when the right to remain silent begins and applies. Any push back is, for the most part, hurried lip service only, grudgingly conceded.

> *"If you have any problems at all,*
> *don't hesitate to shut up!"*
> **—Robert Mancoff**

While the police can't be stopped from trying to interrogate you, you do not have to participate in that process. You need only demand, not merely request, a lawyer, say you are remaining silent and say nothing more. Why doesn't the public get it? I suppose one answer is because we're trained very early in life that cooperation is a good thing, answering the police is an act of cooperation, talking fixes everything and confession is good for the soul. Most of us believe that if we don't talk, we will be thought guilty. To that I say, "So what!" Being thought you are guilty doesn't cause your conviction in court. What is viewed on TV is seen as an accurate picture of how the criminal justice system works. TV tells us it works only because we have been conned into thinking so, and therefore don't exercise our rights and just give up.

Police training consists of having an attitude that you are guilty, a confidence in their ability to get you to talk, exploiting your ignorance of your rights, promoting the fear of arrest, and a persistence to press you until you do talk and admit your guilt, or at least admit to facts which will prove your guilt, or, if you don't talk, and are arrested, you are going to jail and will be locked up indefinitely. This attitude and its communication to you is a lie and a ploy to get you to talk, and thereby give up your right to remain silent, and to cause you to think that somehow these things won't happen and you'll be better off by talking. It is far better to let the police officer think you are guilty than to prove it to him by talking and testing.

Probably the greatest irony of our criminal justice system is that almost immediately after the great pronouncements of the U.S. Supreme Court in the 1960s, *Miranda* and *Escobedo*, affirming the Fifth Amendment right to remain silent and the Sixth Amendment right to counsel, and continuing to the present, there has been a gradual and progressive erosion of, or carving out of exceptions to, and the active suppression of, these two basic rights of the individual when accused of an offense.

Only passing mention is made of these two important landmark decisions in the books that I have read on the subject of the history of American Law, books about the Supreme Court, or books written by its retired Justices. It seems that our news media, entertainment industry, and the police treat these decisions as inconveniences to be paid lip service to, if mentioned at all, and they glamorize the avoidance of these constitutional rights by the police.

As a result, by the time a criminal charge reaches the courthouse, and plays out in the system, that system seems little more than the inconvenient ritual that must be endured by society so that we can promptly get to punishment, because we have assumed the person charged is guilty, having been conned into admitting to the offense on the street, when they first encountered the police. Even worse, we assume guilt, because someone exercised their Fifth or Sixth Amendment rights. Why did they admit the offense to the police? Because they were unaware of what their rights were, when those rights applied, and how to apply them. The result has been too many people being found guilty on too little objective evidence independently obtained. By the time the case reaches the court, it is very predictably over as a factual matter, and the lawyer hired to defend these cases reduced to begging for leniency. There is nothing technical, mysterious or complicated about what you should do during a police encounter.

> *"You should be more careful about what you say."*
> **—Confucius**

I can hear my critics as this is written. "This guy hates the police, loves drunks, pot smokers, and other criminals, defends their conduct, and advises them on how to break the law and get away with it." Let me dismiss these allegations one at a time.

I hate the police? I counsel an attitude of respect for them, and urge calm and politeness in all communications with them. I recognize their risk taking and advise conduct toward them that reduces their safety concerns. The only negative statements are directed toward the "police method" which consists of the universally recognized and approved practice of deception, manipulation, misrepresentation and any and every trick, tactic and seductive lie in order to get people to talk and give evidence against themselves. Even the police themselves will acknowledge that they do this as a part of their training and job description. That they do this is my merely pointing out what they in fact do, and not a criticism of it.

This is the not-so-secret "dirty little secret" upon which the American criminal justice system heavily depends. A system that starts out with lies, told to you when you are alone with the officer, and you, hoping to avoid arrest, giving in to those lies and doing exactly what will get you arrested; talk and take tests. Then once you talk and test, the police put the system in motion, and arrest you. Every step of the way thereafter, everyone is supposed to tell the truth. The only lies excused are those of the police at the very beginning of the process where their lies cause you to self destruct. In no other place in our system is lying said to be tolerated. In no other law related occupation I am aware of is deception taught as a job technique. If a lawyer lies to the court, he gets disciplined or possibly disbarred. If a witness lies in court, he has committed perjury. If you give false information to the police you can be prosecuted for doing so, but if the police lie, and do it well on the street over time, they get promoted from patrolman to detective. They don't have to lie in court; they just repeat what you said and did on the street. Great system! What's the answer and defense to this institutionalized manipulation and deception by law enforcement? Silence—knowing how and when to be silent and knowing you can be silent.

To say that I like or approve of people accused of the crimes emphasized is to confess ones total misunderstanding of the work of a criminal defense lawyer. It is not the job of the lawyer to like or dislike his client. Although it is preferable to have a likable client, it is not necessary, nor is it the lawyer's job to approve or disapprove of the conduct alleged, nor to judge his client. His only job is to represent the client. In doing so, in "defending" his client, the criminal defense lawyer's principle focus is, and should be, whether or not the prosecutor has enough evidence. Is the government's proof sufficient for a conviction? That is the question. If the lawyer judges anything, it should be only the quality and quantity of the prosecution's evidence, hopefully, none of which was served up to the police by the client, because he or she was unaware of their right to remain silent, and when it begins.

The problem with the public's perception of what we lawyers do is the word "defend". It has a meaning to a lawyer quite different from its popularly understood meaning. We don't "defend" your conduct; we "defend" you against improper proof or insufficient evidence of guilt. Do I approve of irresponsible alcohol consumption or pot smoking? I do not. This is not the issue, nor the question. I approve of a properly working criminal justice system. I do not, have not, and cannot, within the code of professional responsibility, nor ethically, counsel in how to break the law. My counsel and advice begins once the accusatorial process, the police encounter, has begun, which assumes the crime has already been committed, and its investigation has begun, or at least the police think so.

Because of the determined and persistent effort of the police to suppress and circumvent our knowledge, as well as the media's conscious or unconscious distortion of our knowledge and understanding of these rights; until this has changed, or been counterbalanced, justice, as the law system intends it, is not done.

Many years ago, I heard and saw in print a very able prosecutor who I opposed many times in court say when commenting to the media that when the trial jury acquits, the system has failed. I always have and still do sharply disagree with such statements and ideas. If a court or jury does not convict, it is the prosecutor who has failed to meet the constitutional standard and burden, not the system failing. If the process works as it should, justice is done by an acquittal as well. Since the prosecutor's office in Virginia is political, they are elected, it is not surprising that a prosecutor would not blame an acquittal on his or her own failure in court, particularly when commenting to the news media on such a result.

Although the constitutional right to remain silent and have the assistance of counsel applies in all criminal cases, from the most minor offenses for which jail can be imposed, to the most serious, the perfect offense to serve as a teaching vehicle for the Fifth Amendment is the offense of Driving While Under the Influence (DUI), a misdemeanor offense with major consequences. I can think of no other offense so widely charged, so frequently heard in court, or so likely to produce self-destruction by those pulled over for this offense, nor so burdensome for so long afterward to those convicted, and no other offense for which so many people are convicted on relatively little evidence gathered from sources other than from what comes out of their mouth, evidence needlessly given up by "abdication through unawareness". This is the offense focused on. This offense accounts for one in ten of the twelve million cases heard annually across the country.

DUI and possession of marijuana are notable offenses in a number of respects. They are probably, after minor traffic infractions such as red light violations, running stop signs, and exceeding the speed limit, the most widely committed serious misdemeanor offenses in the country at this time. Together they account for approximately 2.1 million arrests, nationwide, according to the latest U.S. Justice Department figures I've seen, the year 2012. Those who get accused of these offenses can be found in every segment of society, they are committed by rich and poor, men and women, all ethnic, religious, and racial backgrounds, white and blue collar workers, professionals, executives, housewives, students, and celebrities. The persons who commit these offenses do not regard themselves as criminals, and are often in trouble of this kind for the first time in their lives. They are most often responsible, working people raising families or going to school.

Most significantly, they usually have in mind a great amount of misinformation from friends, acquaintances, or the news and entertainment industry which have, over time, created an expectation of giving in to the inherent coercion of being questioned and the police interrogation process. As a result of this misinformation, when accused, or approached by the police, who suspect these offenses, we say and do the wrong things.

When police officers tell you, in response to you telling them you have nothing to say, it will go easier for you if you talk to them, or have no right to a lawyer because you are not in custody, they are lying. Talking to them makes things go easier for them, not for you. Don't fall for that. It is a lie to get you to talk and give evidence against yourself. Most officers are not used to people they encounter who know and exercise their rights, and may become verbally abusive and start lecturing you, telling you that you're watching too much TV, (Really? You don't get what I'm advising from TV) place you in cuffs and take you to a judicial officer. As will become clear as you read on, this is what you want.

The problem with most officers is that the law they know consists in large part of that law which, from their perspective, allows them, according to their reading of it, to sidestep your rights, or narrow the circumstances where *Miranda* applies and the exact words you must use to let the officer know you are remaining silent, not taking tests, and demanding a lawyer. They will persist in the effort to get you to talk by telling you all sorts of things having a common theme— you don't know what you're doing, or that you're making a mistake when you exercise your right to silence. When you remain silent, you demonstrate that you certainly do know what you're doing, and are definitely doing the right thing.

You don't need to lie, just shut up! You can't lie when you say nothing. The police are pretty much dead in the water when you say and do nothing during your time with them, which you should try to shorten as much as possible to get off the street and to the magistrate, or if free to leave, walk away.

What most people don't realize when they give up their right to remain silent is that they're doing exactly what the Fifth Amendment guarantees that they can't be compelled to do—give spoken evidence against themselves. Virtually all people fear arrest as their principal reason for not remaining silent because they think an arrest becomes a permanent part of their record, a fear much overblown, not necessary, and exploited as much as possible by the police. That fear is cultivated by the police as a part of their training. It is their number one tool to get you to talk. An arrest does not have to remain a part of your permanent record when you plead not guilty and are acquitted of the charge against you. When you plead not guilty, and are found not guilty, in Virginia, and elsewhere, there are provisions of law which allow for the expungement of the record of your arrest. This means everything is erased, the arrest, the charge, the outcome, everything disappears. Your chance of being found not guilty is great when you don't talk and don't test, and thereby don't supply those missing and necessary elements of the government's case against you.

If the fear of isolation by and with a law enforcement officer is not the primary reason for giving up your right to remain silent, probably the most compelling is the fear of arrest. People think that if they give the police the answers they want, they won't get arrested. The exact opposite is almost always the case. Telling the officer you've been drinking, have marijuana in your car, or in your pocket, taking and failing field sobriety tests, is absolutely going to get you arrested. By talking and testing, you will not avoid arrest. You've practically guaranteed it! So, having said everything to the officer the prosecution needs to convict you, what have you accomplished? Arrest **and** conviction. No lawyer can win for you or accomplish anything except perhaps a less severe sentence after begging for you. That is all you've left for your lawyer to do if you run your mouth to the officer instead of exercising your right to remain silent from the beginning.

> *"Men govern nothing with more difficulty than their tongues."*
> **—Spinoza**

Now consider saying nothing other than identifying yourself and you take no breath tests or field sobriety tests. Okay, so you get arrested. It is not the life altering event you may fear it is, or have been misled into thinking. The police want you to think it is, so you'll make a bad decision and talk to them under the mistaken belief you won't get arrested. Decisions made while you are afraid, like decisions made when you are angry are almost always wrong. Any competent criminal defense lawyer will smile broadly when you tell him you said nothing and took no tests, and in fact that turns out to be the case. Trust me, virtually all guilty findings by courts are against people who did not remain silent and were convicted on their own statements, and their cooperation out on the street. Cooperation will get you convicted, and little else.

Arrest is not as terrible as most people think. You are searched, placed in handcuffs, and promptly transported to a judicial officer. Here in Northern Virginia, in the Washington, DC Metropolitan Area, this usually takes less than an hour or two, if you are arrested for a misdemeanor. Your car is towed to a police storage lot and searched if you are stopped while driving. You are released on bond, and after paying a towing and storage fee, you get your car back. You are not beaten, or otherwise abused, you are not kept in solitary confinement, you are not put in a cell with sex offenders or dangerous people. Your arrest is a small price to pay when the alternatives are considered, your certain conviction, a criminal record that stays with you, a fine, and possibly a jail sentence, suspension of your driving privileges, depending on the offence, an ignition interlock on your car, probation, community service, random urine screens, rehabilitation classes, are the seemingly endless and often humiliating terms and conditions of probation.

That's not the worst of it. A conviction record can cost you your job, adversely affect your ability to get future employment, may affect your ability to gain admission to college, join the armed services, own or possess a firearm, work for the government, and enter certain trades or professions. All of this is unlikely to happen if you don't talk, and take no tests because the prosecutor will not otherwise have enough evidence to convict you most of the time.

Despite its originally intended design by the authors of the Constitution and the Bill of Rights to strike a balance between government power and individual rights, our criminal justice system and indeed our society is a failure when it comes to the Fifth Amendment. The system has become lopsided against the individual. The *Miranda* decision, which requires the police to advise persons arrested of their Fifth and Sixth Amendment rights, has been reduced to a hollow, meaningless ritual by the tone and manner of its recitation followed immediately by police questioning as though these constitutional rights didn't exist, have no meaning in the real world and the *Miranda* warnings are just another administrative chore to get beyond. As a result, too many people are being found guilty in court on not much more evidence than their admissions to the police. I know of one local jurisdiction in Virginia where the *Miranda* warnings were once corrupted, in my opinion, by the addition at the bottom of their written *Miranda* warning form of the "right to talk to the police". I must have missed that individual "right" last time I read the Fifth Amendment.

Police tactics include: telling you how expensive hiring a lawyer will be, that you don't need a lawyer if you're innocent and you can handle the matter yourself. No effort will be spared by the police to get you to talk. The more they try, the more you should remember they can't convict you without your admissions or test taking, that they don't have the evidence, and need to get it from you. That's the only reason why they're talking to you. The sooner you tell them you are remaining silent, and are demanding a lawyer, the sooner they will, because the law says they must, stop questioning you and leave you alone.

Driving under the influence of alcohol is perhaps the most serious traffic offense regularly heard in court. Unlike most traffic offenses, which are, for the most part proven almost entirely on the officer's observation, and the offense completed before the officer turns on his emergency equipment to pull you over, DUI is heavily dependent for a successful prosecution upon evidence gathered by the officer from the driver <u>after</u> the traffic stop. Even though modern law enforcement has available to it scientific tools and methods for the detection of DUI and other chemical substance related offenses, it is the traditional method, observation of your mistakes by the officer, which is the foundation of police work in this area of law enforcement. What the officer sees is what determines the first decision he makes; whether to stop you.

In the event he decides to stop you, what he then sees, smells, and hears from you (how you came to a stop, what you voluntarily say, how you say it, answering questions, and/or taking tests), your movements and general appearance, determines his second and most important decision. That decision is whether or not to arrest you. These observations from his senses and what you voluntarily say and do, will be the evidence against you. This evidence, the so-called "odor of alcohol", "blood-shot eyes", general appearance, "slurred speech", or "unsteady on his feet", are usually not sufficient alone or in combination for a conviction, because they are subject to attack by the experienced cross-examiner. When each of these descriptions given by the officer is examined in detail, they fall apart principally because all of these descriptions can and often do have non-alcohol related causes, such as fatigue, allergies, illness, or a past medical history which the officer rarely asks about. When pressed, most officers can't explain these vague general opinion type descriptions in an objective, factual way. In addition, they hardly ever inquire if they see blood-shot eyes, for example, as to what other causes may exist for that condition; and there are many having nothing to do with alcohol.

Consider first the odor of alcohol. There is no such thing. The active ingredient in alcoholic beverages is ethanol, which has no odor. What they smell is the metabolized "other" ingredients of an alcoholic beverage. When pressed, most officers can't tell the difference between the odors of beer, wine, or hard liquor. That is why one of the first things the officer asks on the street when he stops you is, "Have you been drinking tonight?" or "What did you have to drink tonight?" At this moment you are not in custody and the *Miranda* warning recital is not required to be made to you. This means the officer doesn't have to tell you about your right to remain silent. Just because he hasn't recited the *Miranda* warnings at this point, doesn't mean you don't have the right to silence at those first moments of the encounter, or that you have to answer questions like that. **You never have to answer any question except about your identity, nor do you have to admit to anything, or explain anything, or take any test!**

Once you make the first mistake of answering what you had to drink, by saying something like "A couple of beers", "A glass of wine with dinner", or "A cocktail before dinner", you have started on the path to your arrest and conviction, seriously damaged your lawyers ability to defend you, and you have given up a great opportunity for your lawyer to undermine the officer's credibility. The officer can then easily say in court that he smelled an odor of beer when in reality he says "beer" because you said "beer", not because he can tell the difference between the so-called odor of beer and the odor from any other alcoholic beverage. I have seen, and fellow defense lawyers have told me of officers describing in Court the breath of designated drivers they pulled over who drank alcohol-free beer, as having an odor of alcohol. The truth of the matter is cops say it because they have become conditioned to say "odor of alcohol" as part of their police speak litany, and on which they don't get challenged often enough to stop saying it. If you tell him what you drank, his credibility goes up, and your case heads downward. Since studies have shown most officers can't tell the difference in the odor of various alcoholic beverages, they will generally concede that they can't unless you tell them what you drank. **Don't tell them, you don't have to!**

Slurred speech? The less speech you engage in, the less of an opportunity the officer has to observe and evaluate how you speak. In any event, in the hundreds of officers I have cross-examined about slurred speech, not a single one was able to recall, when asked, "What word did my client slur?" Having never heard you speak before this encounter, the officer doesn't know you speak the way you do because of a speech impediment which they rarely ask about. Simply put, he's full of BS when it comes to slurred speech. Likewise, for unsteady on his feet, or stumbled. When pressed on cross examination, no officer has said my client fell down or needed to lean on anything for support. I never pass up an opportunity to ask an officer what my client did when the officer said my client was weaving. Invariably, they answer that the client was changing lanes without a signal. How many of us do that when sober?

Regarding blood-shot eyes, every time I hear that one, I ask the officer if he asked the person stopped about allergies, cold medications, if they came from an environment that irritates the eyes, when they last slept and similar questions. The officers almost always respond that they never inquire along those lines, content to assume it was alcohol causing this condition. The same for "unsteady on his feet". When pressed for the factual basis for such conclusions, the officer often can't answer and falls back on his old reliable "I can't recall" as he was taught at the Police Academy in "witness" class. The point is everything that the police testify about in their standard police speak can be picked apart **except for what you say!** Nothing can fix your admissions, explanations, or test results. When a prosecutor hears what you have said to the officer, it's over and you lose.

Another favorite line of the police is "The process will go easier for you". Nonsense; it goes easier for him. With rare exception, a nighttime traffic stop and the odor of alcohol is going to result in your arrest. Ask yourself then, is it better to be arrested and not give the officer evidence against yourself, or get arrested and provide evidence that the officers' suspicions are correct and will guarantee your conviction? The answer is a no brainer. The alternative to remaining silent, running your mouth, and taking any test will doom your case, even with the world's best lawyer. Your case is over the moment you open your mouth, and start answering questions or giving explanations or taking tests. If you think that cooperating will not result in your arrest, forget it! Arrest is the rule, not the exception. If you think the officer will let you go after you admit to drinking, fail breath tests and fail field sobriety tests, you are detached from reality.

I am not a supporter of drinking and driving. Like you, I know of many tragic cases in which death or serious injury have occurred to people victimized by drivers who were drunk. I support the Constitution and especially the Fifth Amendment. From having defended hundreds of DUI cases, it has been my experience that the officer's testimony as to both the driving behavior observed and his observations regarding the condition of the driver fall into predictable and monotonous word descriptions invariably exaggerating what he sees. These word descriptions and vocabulary choices sound almost mantra like, little more than police lingo that sounds more like a prepared script learned at the police training academy, rather than a description individualized to each case. In addition to their familiar repeated scripts, officers use vocabulary in court that bears no resemblance to normal conversation. For example, I and my fellow defense lawyers rarely hear the normal "I smelled alcohol on his breath". The officer testifies instead, "I detected an odor of an alcoholic beverage emanating from his person". This is contrived police speak, and is pure bullshit, but they never tire of using it and other buzz words which, upon first hearing, seem unassailable, until cross-examination.

It often happens when young people congregate outdoors at a park, ball field, high school event, rock concert, or even a bar parking lot at closing time that police officers, sometimes in plain clothes, will approach you and initiate what appears to be a casual conversation. He may even bluntly ask you if you possess a weapon or drugs. That casual conversation is not casual. It is the start if a deliberate effort for which the officer was specifically trained to get you to begin talking. As soon as you do that, the potential for trouble begins. His objective is to find out if you are in possession of anything illegal, either on your person or in your car, or if you have had something with alcohol to drink. In these circumstances you should just walk away without answering, or immediately but calmly and politely tell the officer you have nothing to say. To any provocative comment of the officer such as, "I smell pot, do you?", if you don't just walk away without replying, you should respond, "Am I free to leave?" If they answer, "No", you are under arrest, even without his use of that word. An arrest occurs whenever you submit to the authority of the officer and your freedom of movement is restricted in any significant way. If they say you can leave, walk away immediately. As in the case when stopped by an officer or arrested, you don't have to answer anything except about your identity, and your choice not to answer the officer does not furnish legal grounds to detain you further.

Some will argue that it is good citizenship to engage in conversation with the police. In my view, good citizenship is knowing and exercising your rights. From the beginning of the legal process to the end of it, that process is not, and was never intended to be friendly or cooperative. It is an adversarial process. Never forget that! When officers are doing their job, they are your opponent, not your friend; when they're talking to you, they're doing their job. Your job is not to answer. That is not to say you should be belligerent in tone, you should just disengage.

I've had occasion in open court to correct judges indirectly who, at the start of a criminal jury trial, in their opening remarks, indicate to the jury that all present, the jury, the judge, prosecutor, and the defense counsel are working together. This is absolutely wrong! I correct the judge indirectly by indicating to the jury in my opening statement, "We're not working together, we are working simultaneously, but not together. Never together". Everyone in that courtroom has a distinct and different function. I do not, in the courtroom, ever work with the prosecutor. I work against the prosecutor. In an adversarial system, we are not co-workers, but opponents. Any defense lawyer who works with the prosecutor in the courtroom in the jury's presence during trial is guilty of malpractice, in my opinion. I am cordial to the prosecutor, and professional to everyone in the courtroom, but that's it.

It's no surprise that many people succumb to the persuasion, trickery, misinformation, and overt intimidation by the police, combined with the probable unfamiliarity with the circumstances in which they find themselves when stopped by the police, as well as their intimidating appearance, and the unjustified fear of arrest. To begin with, consider their appearance. Most modern police in urban areas are well dressed, smartly dressed, and conspicuously well-armed. When they approach your car after a traffic stop, they are indeed imposing figures of government authority for a number of reasons. First, they are standing next to your driver's door as you are seated. They seem huge as they tower over you. Second, from this position, you can easily see the formidable assortment of hardware on their belt, approximately at your eye level; a firearm, handcuffs, chemical spray canisters, radios, perhaps a Taser or electric shocking device and ammunition clips—a very intimidating display. Third, when they begin to conduct the business for which they stopped you, they usually speak in a stern, commanding tone, telling you what to do. The natural reaction to this intimidating display is for you to attempt to reduce the tension you feel by "cooperating" which initially takes the form of answering questions. No matter what question he begins with, you should immediately identify yourself, either verbally or by handing over your license, immediately preceded by taking your hands off the top of your steering wheel, or asking the officer's permission to reach for your identification and registration, telling him where it is.

These modern police officers are also well disciplined. They are not supposed to get angry when in response to doing their business with you, you must do your business with them, politely, calmly, respectfully but firmly and clearly. Your business is not to be intimidated, tricked, or manipulated into giving up your right to remain silent, except to identify yourself. Keep both of your hands plainly visible on the top of the steering wheel, where they should be as he/she approaches, and as motionless as possible. If the roadside encounter continues beyond this brief time, especially after you receive a citation or warning, or particularly in the nighttime, be ready with the all-important "Am a free to leave?" If you get any answer other than "Yes", you know what to do and say. "I have nothing else to say, take me to the magistrate right now." Most competent officers will tolerate your remaining silent and not testing, as long as you do it agreeably and with civility, politely and respectfully, clearly and firmly.

PART III

A NATION OF TALKAHOLICS WHO LOSE IN COURT

> "Wise men talk because they have something to say, fools talk because they have to say something."
> —**Plato**
>
> "Words . . . are the money of fools."
> —**Thomas Hobbs**

The American people are obsessed with the right of free speech. It is the first of the Bill of Rights, most exalted of our rights, most zealously protected, and a calling card of our society. A significant part of the history of our country has been devoted to the development of technology to facilitate and expand our ability to speak and communicate. Newspapers, telegraph, telephone, radio, television, recording devices, computers, smart phones, the Internet, Facebook, e-mail—all have expanded and encourage communicating and speaking to one another. We love this stuff and always have. They have become our First Amendment free speech toys and gadgets. We are addicted to using them and what we can do with them.

One beneficial use of these electronic devices has been, in the Fifth Amendment due process context, the recording of police encounters with video capable smart phones. With increasing frequency we see on TV news and talk programs the showing of amateur videos taken by witnesses to police encounters, and not surprisingly, police misconduct. Few things are more irritating to a police officer than the video documentation of their misconduct, if any, during routine stops, by eyewitnesses who are not the persons with whom the police have official business; passengers in the stopped vehicle or bystanders. Police reaction to this lawful video recording is nearly always unlawful, ranging from threatening to, or actually arresting the non-involved person taking the pictures, seizing from them their picture taking device, pushing and shoving them away, ordering them to stop under threat of arrest without other justification, or otherwise preventing the pictures from being taken, such as a back-up officer blocking the camera lens with his body or police vehicle. All of these police actions are due process violations by reason of the police intentionally preventing the collection, on behalf of the person stopped, of exculpatory evidence; that evidence which is favorable to the defense of any charge brought, which may show reasonable doubt of guilt, or undermine the credibility of the officer. The remedy in court when a denial of due process is shown by this sort of police misconduct is, as it should be, dismissal of the charge. Denial of due process is denial of fundamental fairness, the essence of due process. The message—take videos whenever possible and tell the officer that this is what you have asked or told your passenger or bystander to do. If the officer prevents this from happening in any way, you have the start of a good due process basis for dismissal of any charge.

What we don't realize or appreciate is how costly the exercise of free speech is, and how much trouble it causes. Free speech during a police encounter is a disease, an addiction whose only cure is no speech, silence. The Fifth Amendment right to remain silent at such times is your only safe haven. Free speech at such times is the opposite; it is your downfall. The right to remain silent is virtually absolute. Yet when the police are encountered, people who claim to know their rights too often don't have a clue that this is the time to forget free speech, and not to speak.

One of the worst things you can do is to think you can try to talk yourself out of an arrest if officers gives any indication that they smell alcohol or pot. There are instances when this happens, and they may make good anecdotal stories in the office. The fact that someone is a good storyteller doesn't make these occasions less rare or more plausible. As a practical matter, it doesn't happen!

The predominant reason people are imprisoned in our society is they talk. Why do they talk? They just like to talk or they think they can talk their way out of a problem. Often they can, but rarely with a police officer. Theologians say it's good for the soul. Psychologists and prosecutors say it's because the accused wants to explain himself when confronted by authority figures. In my view, based on interviewing thousands of clients, people talk because they don't know that they don't have to say anything, or think they will look guilty if they remain silent. They feel intimidated in the coercive environment of being stopped and questioned. They think the Fifth Amendment's guarantee that no person shall be compelled to be a witness against himself is something they heard about, but has no practical use or relevance in their lives. Once you identify yourself, you don't have to speak, you don't have to admit or explain anything, you don't have to consent to any search, you don't have to take any test, you don't have to cooperate or participate in any police investigation or interrogation by speaking. When a police officer approaches you, nothing is more useful or relevant.

When you talk, and thereby get convicted, you prolong the agony of being involved in the system. Trust me, it is agony. The result, if you lose after hiring a lawyer and defending yourself, is no worse than caving in and pleading guilty because you had no choice because you wouldn't shut your mouth. Any officer that tells you the judge will hold it against you if you don't cooperate (give up your right to silence) is lying! Judges don't penalize people for exercising their right to a trial and making the prosecution prove its case. In fact, many judges I know have told me they appreciate a trial by two lawyers who know how to try a case. It is a refreshing break from the monotony of hearing guilty pleas all morning. By exercising your right to remain silent, the prosecution is much less likely to prove its case against you. More often than not, they have no case when you remain silent and take no tests. The idea that your running your mouth will get you a break with the judge in a DUI case is foolish. The judge cannot and will not ignore the evidence you supplied of your guilt. What you admit to is universally regarded by the law as the strongest possible proof against you, evidence you don't have to provide. Confession is fine in church, but not during an encounter with the police.

When a police officer tells you that he will tell the judge you cooperated or it's better for you if you cooperate, he is making an empty promise. I have never seen a judge be harsher with someone who remained silent. Judges do take into account, however, any rudeness or foul language to the officer. This is usually the only pre-court misconduct seen, and it always hurts your case and your lawyer's ability to help you. Any other misconduct on your part could result in criminal violations and additional charges. Foul language to the officer is constitutionally protected (First Amendment) free speech, but it is always a dumb thing to do. It may make you feel good at the moment, but does not help after that.

Even with the *Miranda* warnings being given, people still talk. The folks who talk screw themselves because they don't know they can say nothing even before or after being advised of their *Miranda* rights. Despite *Miranda*, and the Fifth Amendment, the police still get you to talk in most cases. In my view, people still talk after the *Miranda* warning because, as presently phrased, it is inadequate and is inconsistent and misleading on its face. Its opening line ". . . right to remain silent." is practically cancelled out by the balance of the warning's emphasis on the opposite of silence, the police questioning process; that questioning you and your answering is going to happen, provided you demand a lawyer and one is made available. With a competent criminal defense lawyer present, that questioning and answering process will not happen. In addition, it is not specific enough about the consequences of not remaining silent. Its language is too bland and neutral, as one would expect coming from the neutral judges who chose the words which are then delivered to you by a police officer at the moment you are being handcuffed. As you are being told you are being arrested and are stressed thinking about what's going to happen to your kids, your job, etc., what the officer is saying to you is not sinking in. This is the moment of greatest vulnerability to police speak, and critical mistakes are then made by you.

The *Miranda* warning should sound like it comes from a defense lawyer because it is legal advice to the accused. Your lawyer is not and should not sound neutral. Instead of just blandly advising that anything you say ". . . can and will be used against you in court . . .", it should emphasize the main consequence of talking. As it is now worded, it simply indicates what you say is just another piece of evidence. What you say is always the centerpiece of the case against you—the strongest evidence there is. Given its bland, neutral tone and facial contradiction, as presently worded, it is no surprise that people still talk and get convicted over ninety percent of the time. The warning should go something like this: **You can and must shut your mouth now and keep it shut or you will lose. Do not answer any questions by the police at any time. Demand to speak to a lawyer, say you are remaining silent, then stop talking.**

The police have been very successful doing an end run around *Miranda* by manipulating you to talk before it applies. Immediately following this Supreme Court decision in 1966, it was feared by the police that these constitutionally required warnings would have dramatic impact upon police work, and lower the ninety percent conviction rate. This has not been the case. It has been a false alarm, as the police quickly learned, and continue to sidestep *Miranda* by pre-custody deception. The ninety percent guilty plea rate has remained consistently at that level. Police deception is alive and well.

This continuing high guilty plea (conviction) rate is due to our misplaced focus on the *Miranda* warning for the past half century, and the entertainment industry making its name a household word. This misplaced focus on *Miranda* has, in a sense, been a disservice to the public. As seen on TV, and in motion pictures, *Miranda* comes into play only at the time of arrest, and the warning's opening line . . . **you "have" the right to remain silent** . . . clearly leaves the impression, as nearly all of my clients have told me, that the right to silence starts at the moment of arrest, and not at the time of the stop; that the right to silence is prospective only, from the point of arrest only, suggesting that you cannot remain silent before arrest, when you first encounter the police and/or the right to remain silent does not exist until the point of arrest and the *Miranda* warnings are given. The focus has been on waiting for the police recital of the *Miranda* warnings, as though what you say and do before being so warned during the interval between the initial stop and contact with a police officer and your arrest doesn't count. **It sure as hell does!** It is during this interval, this portion of the encounter, that the damaging statements and test taking are made in pre-custody interaction with the police.

If you are then arrested, and in custody, this is when the warnings are hurriedly recited, with a tone of annoyance at having to do so. **Too late!** The truth of the matter is that you "had" the right to remain silent from the outset, and the arresting officer's recital of the warning to remain silent is pointless if you had not kept your mouth shut and took tests in that critical interval between the initial encounter and arrest. Once you open your mouth to speak, take tests, and admit or explain things (cooperate) in that interval, you've done fatal, irreparable damage to your case and you get **convicted**!

The correct focus should be on the Fifth Amendment right to silence, which you "had" available at all times, and particularly at the moment of first contact with the police. To "have" the right to silence as the *Miranda* recital states, suggests a time and a starting point of your right to silence, which is different from "had". This is the myth, the mirage, that *Miranda* is the great savior to the accused. **It is not!** By the time you have heard the *Miranda* warnings, you blew it at the beginning of the stop by the police. Its message is that your rights begin at and after arrest, which is totally false. Law and order TV tells us that our rights begin with the click of the cuffs, and this is the greatest deception of all. The great savior is silence at all times.

No one should, after high school, need reminding of the absolute right to remain silent. This is self-preservation, one of the most instinctive and most basic of all human responses to danger. *Miranda* is one of the great landmarks of American Constitutional law. The problem with it is not what it means or stands for. The problem is how our popular culture has emphasized it, and virtually ignored the right to silence before the point of arrest. The shield of *Miranda* is post arrest in its application. In the hands of the police, it has become pointless, a virtual closing of the barn door after the horse escaped.

The *Miranda* warnings are only required to be given to persons in custody, and who the police want to question or interview. You are not in custody when an officer stops you in traffic or walks up to you on the street. The surest way to tell if you are in custody is ask the officer if you are free to leave, as soon in the encounter as you can, and keep asking until you get an answer. Whether or not you are in custody, you do not have to answer any questions, reply to any statement, or do anything other than to identify yourself. The police want you to think that you have to talk to them. They are **wrong**. Whether or not you are in custody, and whether or not you are given your *Miranda* warnings, the Fifth Amendment always applies. The Fifth Amendment right to remain silent and not give evidence against yourself does not go away unless you consent to waive its protection and talk. The Fifth Amendment is your absolute bottom line round-the-clock protection against the government and its agents, the police, and police pressure to talk. *Miranda* simply is a reminder of your rights, it does not create them. The Constitution does that. When you talk, and cooperate you get nothing in return except trouble. Don't make the mistake of intimidating yourself by thinking that if you don't answer and don't cooperate, the officer will think you're guilty or hiding something. That's what he thinks to begin with and that's what he wants you to think under the false notion that if you talk and provide incriminating facts, you will thereby avoid arrest. You will not.

It is during this pre-*Miranda* interval that the seduction, disinformation, manipulation, and deception by the police, takes place and has its devastating effect on your fate in court. This is the interval that is not covered by *Miranda,* but definitely covered by the Fifth Amendment. This is when the officer puts to work his training to be either the authoritarian tough guy, using fear and intimidation to get you to talk, screw yourself, and lose in court, or the smoothly conversational "nice guy" with whom you've been "cooperating", talk, screw yourself, and lose in court. Your response to either approach or technique is what determines what happens to you at the courthouse.

We have been conditioned during our formative years by our parents and our teachers, and as adults by our popular culture to talk things over, cooperate, work out our differences by talking, and to explain ourselves to authority figures. What we have either never learned or have forgotten is when to shut up, and to whom not to talk. **It's the police.** Talking to and cooperating with them is a disaster for you and your case. When you call upon the police for help, they're great. When they call upon you, watch out! When they call upon you, nothing serves you better than silence.

During some encounters, the police may tell you as part of their investigation and, to get you to speak, that they have lots of evidence against you, coupled with, "If you didn't do anything wrong, you don't need a lawyer." Your response should be, "Then you don't need to talk to me. I demand to speak to a lawyer right now," and end with, "I have nothing else to say". Everyone is familiar with the often repeated mantra, "The police have a right, indeed a duty, to investigate and uncover criminal activity" from the most minor traffic offense to the most serious felony. Prosecutors repeat it regularly, in argument to judges. It is so often heard, it is almost comforting to hear it coming from the law enforcement community. It is good to know they're on the job. Whenever I hear it in court, I reply to the judge the opposite, equally true, and equally absolute right of the person being investigated, accused, suspected or under arrest, of the right to not participate in that investigation by answering questions. If a prosecutor makes such a comment to a jury, implying a corresponding duty to cooperate in that investigation by talking, it could cause a mistrial, depending on the words used, because the right to silence or wanting legal counsel cannot be commented upon. There is no penalty or downside for exercising the right to silence.

Interrogation or what they now deceptively call being interviewed is not limited to questions by the police. It includes any statement by an officer in your presence or within your hearing, intended to obtain a response from you, or draw you into a conversation. One of the classic techniques that tricks you and draws you into talking is for two officers to talk to each other about your case within your hearing, and say something deliberately false in the hope that you will interrupt and correct what they said with something damaging to your case. Indeed, the catalog of investigative techniques is long and varied, with two common themes; they're intended to get you to talk and are invariably false. Lying in police work is permitted and tacitly approved of because it's believed widely in government and in law enforcement to be the lesser evil in the choice between the evil of letting a crime or infraction go unpunished for lack of evidence, or the evil of lying to obtain that evidence for a conviction.

In response to all the time and effort expended to get you to talk, you need only to remember and say, "I have nothing to say. I demand to speak to a lawyer." The entirety of the police's technique boils down to this approach; we have the evidence, we know you are guilty, we know you did it, we need to hear your side, you have a right to talk to us, tell us your side. These two last lies being the most sinister of all the lies they tell. If any of those statements were true, the police would not need to talk to you. The sole purpose of these lies is to get you to give the police the facts that they don't already have or know. Don't fall for it!

Another very tempting lie that the police utilize is that "Things will go easier for you" if you talk or they will get your charges reduced or dropped. These are more lies. Only a prosecutor can reduce or drop charges, and a police officer can't commit or obligate a prosecutor to do anything. Any such agreement between the police and you, even if in writing, is worthless. The only promise or agreement you can rely on is one made by the prosecutor with your lawyer. Only those two can and should agree for you after the prosecutor has made a full disclosure of his evidence against you to your lawyer. Only then with your lawyer present, and with his concurrence to do so, should you say anything. Your statements will be probably given under a grant of immunity that your lawyer has negotiated for you, in exchange for your statement, if your lawyer has done his job correctly. Only after you know, understand, and agree in writing to the bargain your lawyer has negotiated for you, should you then speak, with your lawyer present and then only to the prosecutor. Such agreements will, if your lawyer knows what they're doing, usually include in exchange for what you know and say, dropping charges, reducing charges to less serious offenses, not bringing other charges, recommending to the court a particular sentence, or immunity from prosecution for offenses you disclose or agree to talk about.

If what the police officer collects through his senses of sight, hearing, and smell were enough to make a DUI case against you, there would be no need to get you to talk, have you take tests, or engage in any conversation. Other than the most minor traffic infractions, such as running a stop sign, a red light, or speeding, which the officer sees completed before you ever hear their siren, or see their emergency lights, most other offenses the officer may develop after he stops you are developed against you by what you say and what you do, and nothing else—just you!

Most DUI stops and arrests occur late at night, long after rush hour traffic has subsided and the roads are practically empty. It is then that patrolling officers can see what is little more than the slightest departure from driving perfection, and use these observations as the basis for a stop. These deviations from perfect driving are the typical minor adjustments to your driving necessitated by traffic volume during the day which go unnoticed except at night when the roads are empty. One of the classic (bullshit) excuses for a night time stop is a turn or lane change without a signal. Many drivers overlook the signal when there is no other nearby traffic to be affected by the lack of a signal. The law in Virginia does not prohibit lane changing or turns without signaling unless another vehicle will be affected. Yet this has become one of the most common reasons for an officer to pull you over, especially late at night, and your car can readily be seen by the police as it often is the only vehicle on the road other than the officer's, and you're not giving a signal affects no one. These types of deviations from perfect driving have nothing to do with one's ability to maintain control of the vehicle, but because they are observed at night, they frequently result in a stop by an officer whose mind-set at these hours is that you have been drinking, or are drunk. Before he even sees your car, that's what he's thinking.

After a night time stop, a favored ploy to obtain evidence to use against you is to say, directly, or suggest to you that they simply want to make sure you are okay to drive on to your destination. "If you're okay, we'll let you go", or "You can leave and continue on." Letting you go does not happen if they sense that you had been drinking. They want you to prove you're okay by taking field sobriety tests which prove little and which you will not pass, and the street breath test. **None of these tests are required. You can lawfully choose not to take them.**

The street breath test is just a preliminary screening, using a hand held device the officer asks or directs you to blow into at the time of the stop. It is significantly different from the breath test machine at the police station in several important ways. The station house machine test result is used as proof in court because it is regularly checked, serviced, and certified for accuracy. The handheld device is not. The station house machine has the ability to purge itself of alcohol from a prior use. The handheld device does not. The station house machine gives a precise numerical reading and a printed result of which you get a copy. The handheld device may not. The station house machine measures deep lung air—alcohol in your blood. The handheld device may include and may be influenced by alcohol in your stomach and/or mouth alcohol residue which causes an inaccurate measure of blood alcohol content. It is only blood alcohol that counts. Finally and most importantly, choosing not to blow into the handheld device on the street does not constitute the separate offense of "refusal". You won't be charged with refusal because you did not blow on the street. It is not taking the station house test that results in the separate refusal charge, which won't go very far if your DUI arrest is not valid.

That handheld device is so notoriously inaccurate that it is not generally evidence that is admissible in a DUI prosecution. It is admissible in a refusal prosecution for determining probable cause—the validity of the DUI arrest. Any reading on these hand held breath screening devices on the street will give the officer probable cause for arrest and eliminates your ability to challenge that issue in either charge. **Do not** take this test. **It is not required.**

If you think you can pass the so-called field sobriety tests, try them at home under ideal conditions where there are no flashing police vehicle lights, no traffic generated wind to affect your balance, a smooth surface, no intimidating presence of a uniformed officer who is convinced from the beginning you are guilty, and where there is no fear of arrest. You can't do them at home, so forget it on the street. **Do not volunteer to take them.**

They really are not tests in any meaningful sense. They simply give the officer more to say against you in court. Judges love these details from the officers because the judges then have a place to hang their hat when they decide against you. Many of the buzzword phrases the police use have never been scientifically validated as accurate proof of intoxication, but simply because these buzzwords have been relied upon in thousands of decisions which have reached Appellate courts and therefore become precedents, or authority, judges point to them and rely on them, even though the underlying basis for that authority has not been scientifically validated.

> *". . . silence is the wisest thing . . . to heed."*
> —**Pindar**

The best method to minimize these buzzwords from being spoken in court against you is for you not to provide speech or behavior from which these buzzwords derive; no answers, no explanations, no admissions, no breath tests, no physical tests. Less time between the stop and arrest means less evidence gathering time, less intimidation time, and less coercion time the police will have, because upon your arrest the police must take you to the magistrate without delay.

The two "approved" physical tests according to the National Highway Transportation Safety Administration (NHTSA) are the "one leg stand" and the "walk and turn" tests. Both are voluntary only. In the one leg stand test, you are instructed to stand on one leg of your choice, and then hold the other six inches off the ground. You must hold this position for thirty seconds, with your hands motionless at your sides. You cannot wobble, sway, or move your hands for balance retention. Most officers do this test wrong, because they insist that you count to thirty. That is not how the test is prescribed according the NHTSA police training manual. The officer must time the test with a timepiece, in order to comply with the test protocol and stop the test at thirty seconds, and do it on smooth, level ground.

During trials, I have asked officers to step down from the witness stand and demonstrate some of these so-called field sobriety tests to a jury. Knowing they had nothing to drink and performing them under ideal conditions; a smooth floor, no fear of arrest, in a well-lit courtroom, and being familiar with how to do them, they couldn't with the same precision they expect from you. It should come as no surprise, then, that no one suspected of driving while under the influence can perform such tests at night, on the street, probably for the first time in their lives, amidst the officer's flashing cruiser lights, often on uneven roadside surfaces, after numerous deliberately confusing instructions, rapidly given, and with the genuine threat of arrest. Moreover, with the officer having alcohol on his mind, how can anyone believe they will get an objective or fair evaluation of their performance on such tests from an officer whose sole aim is to build a case against you for the prosecution? In fact, if you ask for clarification of the officers' deliberately confusing instructions, they use that against you as well by writing in their notes and testifying to the judge that you having to ask for clarification is more proof of intoxication or being under the influence, because you couldn't follow their "simple instructions". You can't win, no matter what you do, unless you do and say nothing.

In the walk and turn test, again without using your arms for balance, you must keep them at your side, and walk nine steps often along an imaginary line, heel touching toe, and at the end of the first nine steps, pivot and return along the same imagery line, taking nine steps heel to toe. The NHTSA protocol specifies an actual line. How can you possibly stay on a line you can't see, at night, on a poor roadside surface? **You won't pass this test either.** Don't do these, or other non-approved tests, such as counting backwards, reciting the alphabet, touching the tip of your nose, fingertip touching . . . **no tests, period!** The only activity I know of that requires walking heel to toe is a tight rope (high wire) walker employed by a circus.

There is a third NHTSA approved standard test called Horizontal Gaze Nystagmus (HGN). In this test the officer holds an object such as a pen vertically at eye level in front of you and moves it from one side of your head to the other, telling you to follow the movement only with your eyes. At the extremes of lateral movement of the eyeball it vibrates or shakes to some degree when that eye position is held. This test is the most suspect of all because, again, most officers do it wrong—not as the protocol demands, and most significantly, Nystagmus is a medical condition, has dozens of causes having nothing to do with alcohol consumption, and no officer I've encountered has had any or sufficient medical training to be competent to testify to this medical condition. For that reason many judges correctly give little or no weight to the HGN test. Notwithstanding its worthlessness, you should not participate in this voluntary test either.

Most officers do not conduct these tests correctly as prescribed by their training, because, in the walk and turn test and the one leg stand test, they are allowed to vary the location for "officer's safety" considerations, and do so by picking bad surfaces such as roadside shoulders. Officer's safety is another buzz phrase which causes judges to tune out any cross examination which points out the officer's incorrect administration of the test as a possible basis for your imperfect performance. Performance perfection is what they expect without telling you, and the slightest imperfection is viewed and described as total failure. They will try to talk you into taking these tests under the false promise to let you go if you pass. You are not going to be let go, because you're not going to pass, and all you've accomplished is to give the officer what the judge accepts as proof of being under the influence, as supposedly shown by your lack of muscle control or coordination, on these impossible to pass exercises or so-called tests. These tests were developed by law enforcement for law enforcement, and do not meet levels of validity required by the scientific community, even when the officer "goes by the book", and conducts them as the NHTSA training manual prescribes. Studies repeatedly show officers are wrong after administering these tests over forty five percent of the time with the number of false arrests of sober individuals approaching one out of four. Even the most vocal proponent of these tests concedes that they demonstrate only a probability of impairment, not proof beyond a reasonable doubt.

Message—you are doomed to failure no matter what, in the eyes of the officer, you do, and worse yet, these so-called tests have little to do with your ability to control a motor vehicle. Yet when a judge hears the officer's description of how poorly you did, this is just more evidence which tunes out many judges to anything else in your favor or that the officer may recall that was consistent with sobriety, inconsistent with intoxication, and you get convicted. These things he does not write down because they don't help the prosecution.

Even if you manage to do what you think is well on these tests, what you did well or correct will not be recorded by the officer, and therefore not recalled at the time your case goes to court. Why won't he record what you did well? Because he is trained not to. He's trained specifically to write down in his notes and report what evidence is "available to establish the essential ingredients of the prosecutor's case", according to the NHTSA Instructor's Manual for training in DUI detection and testing. This is the standard teaching tool for this work in law enforcement. Nothing is mentioned about recording what you did correctly other than the vague generality of making sure the officer's report for the prosecution is complete. Complete, to a defense lawyer means content which includes what you did consistently with sobriety. Complete, to the officer means content which has nothing in your favor.

Moreover, these tests are usually done after alcohol is mentioned to the officer by you. How can the officer possibly not be influenced in his judgment of your performance on the test after noticing alcohol or what he claims or thinks is alcohol, or worst of all, is told by you that you had been drinking? Plainly and simply, you will fail these tests according to the officer, and he will so testify. As long as these tests are voluntary and you are not required by law to take them, don't. They're screwing you over, and they know it!

The NHTSA instructor's manual for the training of police officers in DUI detection and field sobriety testing flatly states that DUI enforcement is "based on the driving public's fear of being arrested". The manual goes on to say that "unless there is a real risk of being arrested there will not be much fear of arrest". This is what the police are taught; the fear of arrest is what they stimulate and depend on. Can there be any doubt that when they confront you in a nighttime traffic stop situation, that your arrest is their objective? If you agree there's no doubt, then surely it makes no sense to listen to or believe any police suggestion that if you give any evidence by way of admissions regarding drinking, or taking breath or field sobriety tests you will not get arrested. You'll not only get arrested for DUI, you will be convicted in court on evidence you volunteered. The message? Talking to, and testing for the officer who stops you is legal suicide.

Everything that the officer testifies about in their standard police speak can be picked apart by your lawyer except for what you say. Nothing can fix your words, your admissions, test results, or explanations. The officer is so intent on remembering what you said, they write it down in their notes and review what they wrote just before testifying, so that they look credible. That credibility excuses their fall back on cross examination to the old reliable "I don't recall" when it comes to remembering what you did that was consistent with not being under the influence and he didn't write down. This is what they learn in "witness school", a standard part of police training.

Police reports of the incident which resulted in your arrest are written and prepared after the officer knows the results of any tests you take. How objective, then, can these reports be? This is what they use to recall the facts of your case when it comes to court for trial several months later. It should be clear by now that the deck is stacked against you if you hand over evidence to the police by talking and testing.

Many of you are on your way home after consuming alcohol responsibly during an evening out. When stopped, you are not under the influence, because the first alcohol you drank that evening has been absorbed and metabolized and the last alcohol consumed has not yet been absorbed into your bloodstream, nor reached the brain. Many of you would have made it safely home but for being stopped. Many clients tell me that they are very close to home when pulled over; less than a mile is most often reported.

As you are detained by the police at roadside, told the officer you're not discussing what you drank and you won't be taking any tests, then probably arrested, and transported to the magistrate, the absorption clock is ticking; the BAC rising. Then, after approximately one and one half hours, by which time you would have been home and off the road, when what you drank is fully absorbed, and your BAC is at its highest possible level, you foolishly take the station house test and are over the limit. You are then charged with being over the limit back at the time of the driving conduct. This is the trap, the voodoo science, the fraud, the assumption that your BAC was the same when driving as it was when tested one and one half hours later. It is not the same. The reality is actual scientifically valid proof of your BAC at the time of driving is rarely, if ever, presented in court. Even though in Virginia the police station BAC reading only gives rise to a "permissible inference" that the BAC was the same back out on the street and probably below the legal limit at that time of the driving conduct, that argument falls on deaf ears in Court. Only the result of the station house test, which you shouldn't have taken and didn't have to take, is remembered by the prosecutor and many judges, and you lose and are convicted.

If the "standard" field sobriety tests were true standards, there would be support for them in the scientific community and its literature. No credible support exists. A false standard has been created, simply by labeling these field tests standard.

My question is, of what are they a standard? Good and valid science? Reliable indicators of being under the influence? The so-called standard field sobriety tests are neither standard nor meaningful, reliable scientific tests. They are designed for you to fail.

Furthermore, they are not reliable indicators of anything resembling proof of the quality that due process demands. When you take any of these tests, and the officer testifies as to your performance, he is essentially giving opinions and the judge finds you guilty on little more than the officers' opinion; hardly what the law requires. This kind of evidence falls considerably short of proof beyond a reasonable doubt of your condition when operating your vehicle. These field sobriety tests only show, at most, probability of guilt; not enough for conviction, yet people are convicted everyday on such opinions and little else.

There are further compelling reasons for not taking the field sobriety tests. First and foremost, is the high rate of error police officers commit in judging test performance, resulting in many false arrests. Studies have shown that experienced officers, who watched videotape of volunteers known to have had nothing to drink, perform these tests and other routine activities, are wrong forty six percent of the time. These officers concluded that this percentage of those sober volunteers had too much to drink. In three NHTSA funded studies in three different states, the rate of false arrest for DUI averaged over twenty-three percent. In short, these tests are given credibility in court that is unearned, as such error rates fall well below what is expected in the scientific community for validity and reliability.

Many, if not all police officers who may stop you, particularly at night, imply, by telling you to "step out of the vehicle and do some tests for me", that these tests are mandatory. Another lie. They are **not** mandatory. Make sure you do not ask the officer if you have to take them or should you take them. The officer will most assuredly tell you that you must or should do so. Inviting such an opinion from an officer or asking him what the law is, is the second worst thing you could do in this situation. The very worst thing you can do is take any on-the-street field sobriety tests, discuss with the officer what you may have had to drink, or take the street breath test, also known as a preliminary breath screening.

If these so called standard field sobriety tests were a valid measure of your ability to operate a motor vehicle with control, why are they not included in the test everyone takes at the DMV to obtain a driver's license? Your vision is checked, you are given a written exam, and an inspector rides with you for the road test. The inspector does not ask you to stand on one leg for thirty seconds, nor walk heel-to-toe on a line, or any other ridiculous exercise remotely resembling what an officer wants and expects you to do in these standard tests if he suspects you of having been drinking after he pulls you over. Taking these tests for the officer on the street justifies the officer's arrest decision, and kills any chances of you winning in court. They mean **nothing** anywhere else. Don't take them, ever! If the officer decides to arrest you because you didn't cooperate by not taking these tests and you didn't engage in damaging conversation, so be it. An arrest under those circumstances is far better for you when you get to your lawyer's office and later to court than an arrest based on testing and talking.

> *"I have often regretted my speech, never my silence."*
> **—Publius**

Additional reasons not to test: The officer, who stops you, benignly asks, without telling you why, "Do you have any health problems?" Most adults, even if they have health issues that don't prevent them from driving or functioning, answer, "No". This is then followed by the officer assuming that you can take the physical tests that he has in mind, even though he didn't specify what tests at the time that the question was posed. The officer never asks specific health questions that are material to field sobriety test performance, regarding medical conditions that can significantly affect your performance. For example, if you're running a fever, it can give an elevated reading on breath test devices; allergies can cause watery or bloodshot eyes. Sixty million Americans suffer from allergies caused by various plants, foods or chemical substances. Twenty-five million Americans have diabetes. This condition also materially affects the blood alcohol reading. Overweight

Americans, all 100 million of them in the adult population, shouldn't do or attempt these tests. People with orthopedic problems from the hips down, balance problems, neurological disorders, consumers of "over-the-counter" medications, prescription medications—all of these dramatically affect both your appearance, and most importantly, your field sobriety test performance. These also cause wrong arrest decisions by police, aside from their high error rates with sober people who don't have these health issues. Even if you did the tests perfectly, if you asked the officer before attempting them, for a clarification of his instructions, which are large in number, deliberately given by him rapidly and confusingly, as many officers do, he will conclude and testify, and the judge will believe, that an intoxicant, either alcohol or drugs, is the reason you didn't understand him, and not his rapid-fire avalanche of confusing instructions. Thus, the argument goes by the prosecutor, asking for clarification of the instructions is additional proof that you are under the influence. No matter what you do, you will be wrong, and regarded as guilty of DUI. Its heads you lose, tails you lose, according to the police.

Even though most officers do not follow the NHTSA field test protocols, and the reliability of these tests is thereby even more suspect, the results of these tests as reported by officers in court are heavily relied upon by judges to regularly find people guilty on very little, if any, additional evidence. To put it bluntly, you are found guilty on bullshit opinions of officers and no other objective evidence. The only sure way to prevent a judge from hearing and relying on such questionable evidence is for you not to give it to the officer on the street. Despite the official sounding name for these tests, standard field sobriety tests, you should not be misled by the suggestion that these tests meet the ordinary requirements of the scientific method. They do not for a number of reasons. None of these tests were developed utilizing double blind studies, a basic scientific method which eliminates observer bias. The tests have not been "normed" by having them performed by test subjects known to be sober, nor have these tests answered such basic questions as how age or gender affects performance, nor how lack of sleep or having practiced the tests bears on performance. In addition, studies funded by the NHTSA have not appeared in any scientific journals, nor have they been peer reviewed. The test subjects on which NHTSA relies were too few in number, were tested in lighted rooms, and had no fear of arrest, which is hardly the case as with real-life people who are detained at night, and tested outdoors in the intimidating presence of flashing police cruiser lights at the roadside, and at genuine risk of arrest. The end result is that many innocent people get arrested based on this so-called science. It is science only to the law enforcement community, and not the scientific community. Once again, it's expediency masquerading as science. Don't be one of those persons arrested and convicted based on these tests. Don't participate.

Another part of his training is to ask you a divided attention question such as to produce your license and/or registration, and while you are in the midst of doing that, interrupt you with another question, calculated to distract you, to make you look fumbling and confused, and unable to quickly locate these items, which the officer will then record in his notes and testify to the court is another indication of your being under the influence because you couldn't readily do these simple tasks.

All this can be avoided by getting arrested as soon as possible without supplying any of the **Big Four** sources of evidence against you. In order for this approach to work and be successful, **you must not do any of the Big Four.**

1. **No statements**
2. **No Street Breath Tests**
3. **No Field Sobriety Tests**
4. **No Police Station Breath or Blood Tests**

Most of the time, you will get arrested, but occasionally an officer will not want to bother if you demonstrably know your rights and do not serve up a strong case, and he might send you on your way. It does happen, in marginal cases, more often than people realize. Their system does indeed depend on your ignorance of your rights. The system frowns upon people who know and exercise their rights because knowing and exercising your rights makes the government appear less efficient and work harder to convict people.

Consider this training point for officers according to this quote from the NHTSA manual:

Usually it is impossible to obtain a legally admissible chemical test until after the suspect is arrested. In some cases, suspects will refuse the chemical test after being arrested; then the case will depend strictly on the officer's observation and testimony. When making a DWI arrest, an officer should always assume that the suspect will refuse the chemical test. The officer should strive to organize and present all observations in the written report and in verbal testimony in such a clear and convincing fashion that the violator will be convicted regardless of whether the test is taken and regardless of the chemical test result. (Emphasis added)

If that doesn't open your eyes to see what you're up against, during a police encounter, nothing will. There it is, in plain English. This is what the police are trained to do. This is the officer's license to exaggerate without actually lying. He is trained to use word choices to describe your encounter with him so as to obtain your conviction even without any chemical tests, or worse yet, even if you recorded any breath test below the legal limit! Still think you should talk and take any tests? This training, this mindset of the police, is why it is vital to your lawyer's success (and yours) that you do whatever it takes to make your encounter with the officer as short as possible, say as little as possible, and absolutely not taking any tests of any kind whatsoever. You must end the encounter as soon as possible with your prompt release or your prompt arrest. With every second you are in the officer's presence and not under arrest, he is making mental notations and observing you to make sure you ". . . will be convicted . . . regardless of the chemical test result."

Translation: the officer will do his best to get you convicted even with chemical test results below the legal limit by what he says and how he says it. In the final analysis, if you are foolish enough to attempt these tests, your performance will be judged imperfect and a failure, testified to in court as such, and only affords most judges the basis on which to find you guilty, and he or she will.

The **only** exception to not taking the station house test is to take it **only** in the following circumstances:

1. **You have made no statements about drinking;**
2. **You have not taken the on-the-street preliminary breath screening;**
3. **You have not taken any field sobriety tests or exercises;**
4. **You are arrested and are 100 percent positive you have consumed nothing with alcohol in the**

previous twenty four hours; no sugarless candy or gum or anything sweetened artificially, no cough or cold medicine containing alcohol, no mouthwash, no liquor flavored food, absolutely no alcoholic beverage.

Your station test reading should be zero and you should then be released on a summons charging you with the infraction which caused the police to stop you. If that zero reading is followed by a request or a demand, for a blood sample from you, the answer is "**No**".

If you say and do nothing on the street, you may be pleasantly surprised by not having to hear the officer testify because the case against you is so weak, the prosecutor will recognize that weakness and not try your case, but instead, deal it away on favorable or at least tolerable terms.

As mentioned earlier, shocking tragedies have been caused by drunk drivers. But to suggest across the board that everyone who has had a drink or two and then drives is going to do the same thing in the middle of the night on an empty road is assuming too much, so as to justify what has happened legislatively and judicially in response. Many judges just stop listening to a case when they hear certain buzz words or phrases. In their mind, it's over; and the accused is guilty once they hear alone or in combination, odor of alcohol, unsteady on the feet, and could not perform tests. Fortunately, these judges are in the minority, and there is always the right of appeal to a higher trial court where a jury trial is available. Juries are often more attentive to the presumption of innocence, what the officer says on cross examination, and insisting that the proof be beyond a reasonable doubt as the judge instructs them. In addition, jurors may have themselves been caught up in the system or have friends or family members who have been. They probably have experienced drinking responsibly, and then driven a vehicle without any control problems. In other words, they are more likely to identify with a similarly situated defendant than a police officer or lower court judge, find reasonable doubt, and acquit you.

It is only occasionally, at best, that a judge will remember that the offense is being under the influence at the time of the driving conduct, not at the time of testing. Usually, when that station house breath test reading is over 0.08, the threshold virtually everywhere, it is the only fact that the judge remembers. Even though that reading, in Virginia, only creates "a permissible inference", that this reading was the same as when driving, it usually results in a guilty finding and the best lawyer's argument will not cause most judges to have a reasonable doubt even when there is evidence of the driver's behavior that was consistent with being sober at the time of the stop, such as a controlled stop in response to the officers signal, promptly getting out the license and registration, and having a coherent and responsive conversation. In many states, the breath/blood test result of 0.08 or more at the station is conclusive proof of guilt. This is why it is vital to your and your lawyer's success that the encounter with the officer on the street is kept as short as possible, that you say as little as possible, and take no tests. Why give the state the opportunity to unfairly prosecute and convict you with what you say and what tests you take? Give them nothing! No words, no tests, and your chance to win in court or for your lawyer to negotiate a plea bargain more favorable than a DUI conviction is greatly improved.

Since you never have to tell your side in court to gain an acquittal, why then accept an invitation from a law enforcement officer to tell your side on the street? In court your side is not a part of the government's case unless you commit legal suicide by opening your mouth and supplying facts they need, but don't have. A perfect illustration is found in the routine minor infraction traffic stop. Most of us have probably experienced this kind of encounter. Recall the seemingly unfriendly, businesslike officer who pulls you over for a stop sign violation, for example. He approaches in a serious manner, asks for, and gets your license and/or registration, returns to his vehicle and moments later returns to your car, hands you a summons for not fully stopping at the stop sign, asks you to sign the summons, you do so, and then he says you are free to go.

You have said nothing, there has been no conversation about the reason for the stop, and he asks you nothing about what he observed. He just writes a ticket, you sign it, and the transaction is over. Why? Because he has seen all the elements for a successful prosecution of that offense. The offense is complete upon his observation of it and he needs nothing from you to prove it in court. He doesn't need you to supply any element of proof in his case against you by anything you volunteer to say or say in reply to his questions. He doesn't need to question you about what he saw. Once he writes the ticket, it's over. If you think you can undo what he did by talking, forget it. Save it for your lawyer, if you hire one for such a minor offense.

In just about every other type of traffic or criminal case, especially in a DUI case, the officer needs you to talk. In such serious traffic cases like DUI, driving while suspended, or criminal offenses such as possession of marijuana or other drugs, and on up the scale of seriousness and into the felony category, these offenses usually require as an element of proof, knowledge on your part, or in the case of DUI, evidence of alcohol or drugs in your body. The officer can't get the proof out of your mind or out of your body without your consent—your voluntarily giving it to him. To get blood out of your body without your consent he now must get a search warrant, according to a 2013 ruling by the U.S. Supreme Court. He, in turn, gives the evidence obtained to the prosecutor to use against you in your trial.

So if the Constitution protects you from being compelled to open your mouth, and giving them what they need to convict you and it is the prosecutor and only the prosecutor, by that same Constitution, who must prove the case against you, why open your mouth? There is no sensible reason for doing so. You will not avoid being arrested. The only thing you accomplish is helping the Government obtain a conviction against you. How is helping them convict you and then having the judge fine you, and possibly order you to jail, and take away your license to drive a good thing? Law enforcement lies to you when they say or imply that out there on the street is the only chance you will have to tell your side. Your side? You don't need to have a side, but if you think you do, nothing requires you to tell it to the officer on the street or at any time. If you remain silent, and give no evidence to the police on the street, you may never have to tell your side because the prosecution may not have enough proof to convict you. If you have a side, tell it to your lawyer, and **only** your lawyer, and let him decide if it's necessary to let the court hear it. Your lawyer can help you with saying what you have to say with the right words at the right time and only if, in his judgment, you need to say anything at all. Your lawyer will know if the prosecution has sufficiently proven its case. Trust your lawyer's judgment; that's why you hired one to begin with.

In most human activity, we are taught from early life to be fair, hear both sides, be a team player, be cooperative, answer authority figures, and work together. When it comes to the criminal law, this attitude leads only to disaster for you and your case. The Founders who wrote the Constitution decided that in criminal prosecutions, the system shall be unfair to the prosecution, by placing the burden on them and only on them to prove guilt. Your innocence is presumed; that is what due process means in a criminal case. Take advantage of the Constitution, know that simple basic right the Fifth Amendment gives you, and always exercise it. Keep the built-in unfairness in the Fifth Amendment that is against the government where it belongs. Let the Constitution work for you; that is why it exists. The Constitution trumps everything in the law. It is **not** an inconvenient technicality.

> *"Well timed silence hath more*
> *eloquence than speech."*
> **—Martin Tupper**

When I was a new lawyer, I attended a continuing legal education seminar and heard speak who was then and still is viewed by many in our profession as one of the greatest criminal trial lawyers of the twentieth century; Edward Bennett Williams. His observation that I have never forgotten is: the best lawyer in the world can't make evidence that comes out of your client's mouth go away. What your client says is a bell that cannot be unrung. Asking a judge or jury to disregard what you say is like asking them not to smell a skunk let loose in the courtroom.

What you say in those first moments of an encounter with the police is so important in the case against you, that what you say to the officer is rarely forgotten by him because he takes great care to write those things down. Simply saying in court that he's a liar if you disagree with what he says you said rarely works because proving a policeman lied is next to impossible, and an unsuccessful attempt at it is absolute disaster for your case. When it boils down to your word against the officer's, most likely the judge will believe the officer unless what he tells the court is absurd or contrary to ordinary human experience. Though not likely to happen, it does occasionally. I defended a case recently where a judge believed the unbelievable, he accepted the word of an officer which I demonstrated with photographs was false. The officer could not possibly have seen what he said he saw from his vantage point. The best practice, then, is not to say anything about your case to the officer for him to write down and repeat in court.

Another approach the police use to get you to talk is to initiate "small talk". Beware of this slipping into casual conversation about the weather, "How about those Mets", and so forth. This is a loud and clear signal from you to the officer that you are willing to talk and you are then at great risk of their leading you into talking about the incident which brought you into contact with him/her. Don't be fooled, stand your ground and stick to your script; "Am I free to leave?", "I have nothing to say", and "I demand a lawyer to advise me before I talk to you". Any officer that tells you that you can or will help yourself by telling your side is not only lying, he is really saying to himself that you are stupid and he is going to prove it by getting you to open your mouth and say something. Almost always it will be the wrong thing. Always remember that you can't ever say the wrong thing to a police officer when you say nothing!

They might also try to suggest to you that it is your civic duty to cooperate with the police. Translation for this police speak: your civic duty is to confess. Another **big** lie! My reply to that is, your higher duty is to preserve yourself, your freedom, your property, your ability to make a living. Your highest civic duty is to honor the Bill of Rights by availing yourself of its protection, the central idea of which is to limit the power of government and its exercise of power over you. Never forget that the police are agents of the government. When you are prosecuted, the name of your case is the government versus your name.

The police might also try the "take responsibility for your actions" approach. Translation for this police speak: do our job for us, and say you are guilty. This is a variant of the civic duty approach and is another big lie. In the criminal law context, your first responsibility is to yourself, according to the Constitution, and not to the government. The Fifth Amendment right to silence and the Sixth Amendment right to a lawyer are intended to mean that you as an individual are more important than the government because these amendments are limits and controls on the government's power over you.

Prosecution and conviction under our system is supposed to be hard for the government, not easy. The problem with driving under the influence and the tragic cases it produces is that they have resulted in the enactment of bad law. Bad law is that law which makes it easier for the government to convict you on too little objective evidence accepted by courts. Bad law has produced some bizarre, plainly stupid outcomes in court where DUI statutory language and enforcement has broadened and is not limited to driving on a public road or highway, and is interpreted to include your being in control of a vehicle anywhere. People have been convicted for operating while under the influence after being found by the police sitting in their car, parked in their own driveway, drinking and listening to music loud enough for a neighbor to call the police, with no act or intention of driving off their property. I have also represented people who knew and decided they should not drive after drinking in a bar, and at closing time called a cab, and were arrested for DUI in the bar parking lot seated behind the wheel of their car waiting for the cab, again with no act or intention of driving. That's how ridiculous DUI laws have come to be worded and interpreted, and their enforcement has become. Do you still think you should talk, cooperate, and take tests?

Expediency has prevailed over what is fair and scientifically valid in the context of DUI prosecutions. The legislatures have made it easy to convict by allowing trial courts to infer, or, in many states presume, from the BAC at the time of the station house test, that the BAC was the same ninety minutes earlier at the time of the stop. That is when it counts. What counts is what the BAC was at the time of the driving conduct because that is the definition of the offense, not being under the influence when tested ninety minutes later. It takes time for alcohol, after drinking, to be absorbed into the bloodstream where it is eventually circulated to the brain. That's where intoxication occurs. You are not intoxicated or under the influence until that occurs. Alcohol in the stomach does not produce intoxication. Alcohol must reach the brain by way of the bloodstream to do that.

That is why in the commonly seen fact pattern, when someone drinks his last drink and leaves a place where it was consumed, gets into their car, heads home, and on the way gets pulled over by the police, they may not be under the influence of that last drink at this point. Yet, this is when the officer smells the smell he claims to smell and it is downhill for the driver from that point, unless the driver remains silent, and takes no tests of any kind. Until the driver opens his mouth, admits to drinking, and supplies additional evidence over the next ninety minutes by talking, taking the street breath test, performing the field sobriety tests, and taking the station house breath or blood test, the police officer does not have enough evidence for a winning case in court against you. In Virginia, the odor of alcohol, standing alone, is, as a matter of law, not sufficient for a conviction for driving under the influence. Couple that odor with a lane change without a signal and that still is not enough to rise above suspicion or probability of guilt and that too, is, as a matter of law, not enough for conviction.

So, unless you want to be convicted, and have all the oppressive things the system can do to you happen to you, **shut up**, and take no tests. Get arrested as soon as possible, and get to the magistrate, agree to come to court, get home, and call a lawyer. Prevention is the key! Prevent the government/police from having the evidence they need by not giving it to them.

In desperation, the officer that pulls you over and wants you to take the street breath test or the so-called field sobriety tests, to which you have said "No thank you", might say that by taking these tests you can prove your innocence. Don't fall for that crap! You never have to prove your innocence or prove anything else; it's the police, and ultimately their lawyer, the prosecutor, who has to prove you are guilty beyond a reasonable doubt.

Alternatively, he might say to you "If you pass, I'll let you go". This is another lie. **You won't pass.** You will not be let go. You will be arrested, and will have given the officer all the evidence he needs. There is a chance he might let you go, realizing as some officers do once in a while, that he can't overcome your silence and choosing to take no tests. On the other hand, if you are arrested—and this is the most likely scenario—he has very little proof against you. Silence is the key, silence is golden, and silence wins for you because silence cannot be ambiguous or misrepresented and is not useful to the prosecutor against you as evidence.

To underscore the importance of not giving to the police any of what I have called the **Big Four** sources of evidence in a DUI case, I want to share what I witnessed in court recently while observing a veteran criminal lawyer I've known for thirty years try a "refusal" case to a conclusion which was in my opinion surely unfair and unjust, but technically correct because the defendant talked and agreed to take the preliminary breath test and field sobriety tests on the street.

The defendant, a real estate broker was pulled over at night for making a turn without a signal, and was asked by the officer to give a breath sample in a handheld device usually carried by the police, after truthfully answering he had nothing to drink. The breath sample reading was 0.03, clearly far below the threshold of being under the influence, 0.08. The defendant was then asked to perform the field sobriety tests which he was confident he could pass. He, of course, did not pass, and his performance plus the .03 reading was sufficient for probable cause for arrest for DUI.

Justifiably upset that he was brought to the station by the officer, the defendant refused to take the station house breath test; the test all drivers impliedly consent to take, as the law is written, if validly arrested for DUI. You can refuse to take it subject to be being charged with the additional offence of refusal, but you can't be forced to take it. All that is necessary for a valid arrest—not a conviction—is probable cause. Because of the 0.03 reading, indicating only the presence of alcohol, and the so-called field test results, the court found probable cause (factual validity) for the arrest, even though the DUI charge was not brought or prosecuted because clearly, at 0.03, the man was not under the influence.

While on the street, the defendant, when asked by the officer if he had been drinking, truthfully answered "no" and then volunteered that he had put a piece of sugarless gum in his mouth to eliminate smoker's breath. Sugarless gum gets its sweetness from sugar alcohol and that accounted for the 0.03 reading on the handheld preliminary breath test device. The lower court found the man guilty of unreasonable refusal to take the station house breath test and suspended the man's operator's license for the mandatory one year. Under Virginia law, no restricted driving privileges can be given if the conviction is for refusing to take the station house test. Ironically, if this defendant was found guilty and convicted of DUI, he could have obtained a restricted license, because in such cases, the refusal charge would have been traded away or dismissed by the court as Virginia Law allows the judge to do following the DUI conviction. In this case, the defendant was faced with a bad choice; plead guilty to the DUI he wasn't guilty of, to get a restricted license, thus retaining his ability to drive and earn a living, or defend himself and win the DUI but if convicted of the refusal, totally lose his ability to drive. This often happens because prosecutors usually insist on salvaging something from a case. In my view, had this gentleman not made any statements to the officer on the street, not taken the handheld breath test, and not taken the field sobriety tests, nor taken the station house test, (observed the **Big Four**) he would have been convicted of nothing. As it turned out, the refusal conviction was appealed, and a jury found the man not guilty. Lesson? Like we teach our young ones about drugs, "Just say no!" to talking and testing. Translation: **shut the hell up.**

Even if you know you have had nothing to drink, you should not take this street breath test if asked to do so, after a late night traffic stop. I continue to maintain that taking this test is a bad idea for several reasons:

1. **These devices are notoriously inaccurate measurers of deep lung air,**
2. **You don't know when the officer last used it, in an earlier stop, and residual alcohol from that earlier use may remain in the device and elevate your reading,**
3. **They are not regularly calibrated and certified for accuracy,**
4. **They are subject to variations of temperature and humidity, as well as being bumped, tossed, dropped, and otherwise knocked out of adjustment,**
5. **In Virginia, you can choose not to take it, and the law states that the officer "shall" tell you so.**

More importantly, if any reading for the presence of alcohol in any amount is observed by the officer, this leads to the officer asking you to perform the field sobriety tests. It is psychologically bad for you because it leads to more pre-arrest conversation and an attitude of "I've gone along so far, I might as well continue to cooperate. The officer is a nice guy and is treating me okay". **This is a big mistake,** because as soon as you have done and said enough, in the officer's opinion to get you convicted, the officer will turn on you and place you under arrest. I repeat, even if you have had nothing to drink, you should not take any tests, neither the street breath test nor the so-called field sobriety tests.

Some cynical officers will often conclude, even if you blow into the handheld breath test device and the reading is zero or clearly well below the legal limit of 0.08, that your driving behavior, even though quite minor, is from drug use, because of the low alcohol reading, and insist that you be transported to a hospital for a blood sample to check for the presence of drugs. This often happens to those who, to the police, fit into their "drug user profile".

The best way to avoid this is to make up your mind immediately not to take any test and clearly tell the officer you're not going to take any test of any kind. Instead, ask the officer if you are free to leave; if he says yes, leave. When he says no, you're now under arrest and the next and last things you should say to the officer are "I have nothing else to say without a lawyer present—take me to the magistrate right now".

> *"Better to remain silent and thought a fool, than to speak and remove all doubt."*
> **—Abraham Lincoln**
>
> *"When I think over what I have said, I envy dumb people."*
> **—Seneca** (4 BC to 65 AD)

You must, to survive legally, from the outset of the encounter, decide that you're not going to give evidence to the officer in any form and **stick to that decision**. I often try to imagine what the officer would be able to say to the magistrate to justify your arrest if you followed my advice—take no tests, and make no statements about drinking. When asked by the judicial officer what you did, what statements you made, and what tests you took, the officer can only answer that you did identify yourself when asked, and perhaps you didn't signal a lane change or turn. I'm willing to wager the judicial officer would tell the officer to write a summons/citation for the infraction which, upon your signing it, should cause your prompt release.

I have often had clients tell me they knew they could remain silent, but were afraid to insist on their Fifth Amendment right because the officer would "think" they were guilty. My reply to this is, "So what?" He thinks that anyway, and what the police think of you is totally unimportant, soon forgotten, is not evidence, and is far better than the alternative—being found guilty for the sole reason that you wouldn't keep quiet. Opening your mouth and giving them everything to prove you are guilty, particularly statements and behavior they can only get from you, results in a conviction record which is important (not to have) and is **not forgotten**.

The police depend on maintaining control of the encounter by lengthening the time they can talk to you before arresting you, relying on your fear of being arrested and your misguided idea that if you talk and thereby cooperate, you will not get arrested. The best thing for you to do is to either get released, or arrested as soon as possible, if the officer says you can't leave his presence. This is because while you are talking, he's observing you and making mental notes which will then become written notes for him to review and to use against you later in court. This time is relatively unrestricted and unregulated by the law, but you can exercise control by walking away, if free to do so. If not, submit to arrest, and insist on being taken to the magistrate right away.

You exercise control by pressing the officer as nicely as you can with the question "Am I free to leave?" If not, and you are arrested, strict procedures come into play and the officer must do certain things to comply with the law. Those things either end his evidence gathering ability, or curtail that activity drastically; limiting it to his observations only if you haven't stopped it entirely by your silence and not taking tests. After searching you and restricting your movement with handcuffs, the officer, upon arresting you, will first advise you of the *Miranda* warnings, and if you then say you demand a lawyer, he must stop questioning you. The next step is for him to take you without delay to the judicial officer. By this point, however, he may have gathered all the evidence from you that he needs. This is why you must take the initiative and tell the officer you have nothing to say immediately upon your sensing that he suspects you of or starts asking about drinking or possessing pot. If that is on his mind, you will not be leaving the encounter without handcuffs. You will be arrested, no matter what you say or do, so be mentally ready and say and do nothing!

There are rare anecdotal exceptions, war stories, that people love to talk about at the office water cooler, but you generally can't rely on these rare exceptions to risk saying and doing the wrong thing on the street, hoping to get lucky. The longer you engage with the officer, the greater his or her opportunity to hear you speak, smell odors (whether real or imagined), observe your appearance, your physical condition, and your movements. These are all components of the definition of intoxication or under the influence. The less time you spend with the officer, the less opportunity there is for such observations. When the officer arrests you, he's got many other administrative chores to deal with, such as searching you for weapons, handcuffing you, dealing with your passengers, if any, and arranging for the removal of your vehicle from the street. Even though he can radio for assistance, and usually does so, he is focused on more than just you. That focus on you is reduced further when you let him know you insist on a lawyer, are not taking any tests, and have nothing else to say. When he knows he won't get evidence from you he must move on in the arrest process. At this point he may begin the usual song and dance effort to talk you out of your position. Your reply should be, "Take me to the magistrate now.", and don't change your position about not talking or not taking any tests.

Courts everywhere are making inroads on the Fifth Amendment's applicability to field sobriety tests on the basis that the physical components of these tests are "non-testimonial"—do not involve the accused speaking, as the Fifth Amendment is interpreted to mean. The spoken word is what it protects—compelled speaking. So long as the tests are voluntary and the choice not to take them carries no penalty, **don't take them**. You cannot be forced to take them. The worst that will happen is that you will probably ensure your arrest, based on officer frustration or irritation, not evidence, **but so will taking them and you'll still get arrested**. And you will have done fatal damage to any chance of winning your case.

Many of my clients explain their talking to the police at roadside as the best and quickest way to "get it over with". **Wrong.** Giving evidence against yourself to the officer will get it over with no sooner than a year on the assurance that you will be convicted, and ordered into the post-conviction bureaucratic meat grinder. If you really want to get it over with as soon as possible, remain silent, take no tests, promptly get arrested, and released on bond. Your case will come to court in about two or three months, and given the strong probability you will win because of your silence, that's how to get it over with.

Remaining silent shortens the process dramatically because remaining silent gives you and your lawyer the best chance to avoid conviction and the agonizingly long post-conviction process of dealing with the overwhelmingly bureaucratic government superstructure that has been set up for those convicted of these offenses. This long post-conviction ordeal is, in most states, for a first conviction, a year-long interruption in your life consisting of an oppressive combination of: restricted driving privileges, ignition interlocks on your vehicle, community service, rehabilitation classes, increased insurance premiums, possible job loss, and a criminal record; as well as, fines, possible jail sentences which are partially suspended and hanging over your head. None of this happens if you win in court, because you kept your mouth shut, did not cooperate, and didn't take any tests.

When I say you'll probably win in court, if you remain silent, I mean that your lawyer should win your case. Everyone charged with DUI or drug possession should hire a criminal defense lawyer. This is so because the laws pertaining to these offenses have become very expansive and detailed and only someone who deals with them regularly is competent to wade through their many fine points and handle your fact pattern correctly in the courtroom. Lawyers learn very early in their careers that anyone who represents themselves in such cases has a fool for a client. The mess they make representing themselves in the lower court where their case is first heard is nearly impossible to fix on appeal.

While urging everyone charged with these offenses to hire a lawyer may seem self-serving, hiring a lawyer is penny-wise; going it alone and representing yourself is pound-foolish. The criminal law business is highly competitive, and most criminal defense lawyers now advertise a free initial consultation. You should take advantage of that fact and shop around. Fees, experience, comfort level, and competence vary considerably. The out of pocket financial cost of losing your case is probably twice to three times the cost of winning with a hired lawyer; and that's only the out of pocket costs. The indirect costs are much higher when loss of driving privileges, possible loss of employment, a criminal record, and all the other consequences already mentioned are taken into account. The inconvenience the legal system puts you through if you are convicted is almost unbelievable and comes with the price of the threat of jail and fines for non-compliance with this regimen of penance and control of your life for at least one year.

Regularly, in an effort to make these laws more strict, more severe and comprehensive, usually in response to a tragedy involving multiple deaths and alcohol, the legislatures of the states amend their DUI laws. In Virginia, it is practically an annual ritual. Therefore, while what I say here is generally good advice, and will stand you in good stead most of the time, you should always seek the advice of counsel if you need to know the current state of the law in your jurisdiction. However, never doubt you always can choose to remain silent, admitting nothing, explaining nothing, taking no tests, and demanding to speak to a lawyer before talking to any law enforcement official. This is the law everywhere and it does not change. Leave no doubt whatsoever in vocalizing your decision, and don't change your mind no matter what the police tell you or threaten you with. The most they can do is arrest you.

Few police officers, prosecutors, or judges believe in responsible drinking. To them, any alcohol consumed means you're drunk. They pay scant attention to absorption rates, burn-off rates, and over what time the alcohol was consumed, as well as your body weight. All of these factors bear on the question of whether a person is intoxicated or under the influence, according to the scientific community and the criminal defense bar, but not to the police or the prosecutor or M.A.D.D. Consequently, far more marginal or even doubtful cases get thrown into the system than should be the case. Responsible drinkers are intelligent enough to pace themselves and drink responsibly, yet when it comes to knowing their most basic rights and taking advantage of them, they are totally irresponsible. It's unbelievable what intelligent people say to me as the excuses for running their mouths, taking tests, and making my job defending them next to impossible, for those reasons only.

Lawyers rarely make guarantees, but three things I can guarantee are:

1. **That the police will try non-stop to get you to talk, take tests, let them search,**
2. **Anything and everything they say to persuade you to give up the protection afforded by the Fifth Amendment is a lie,**
3. **That you will lose in court if you don't remain silent, and say no to tests and searches.**

If you are afraid that not talking to the police officer who stopped you, other than identifying yourself and not taking tests on the street, will furnish grounds for the officer to arrest you, put that notion out of your head. While not talking and not testing may be immediately followed by the officer arresting you, rest assured that such an arrest is not legal, because it has no objective basis in fact or if it does and is for a minor traffic infraction, he must, in Virginia and other states, release you once you sign the summons. The exercise of your Constitutional rights may piss off the officer and precipitate your arrest, but it is not legal grounds for that arrest. The police want you to think that this form of being uncooperative is grounds for your arrest. In fact and in law it is not. On the other hand, even if the arrest is arguably legal, your silence and not testing will stand you in good stead when your case comes to court.

> "An inability to stay quiet is one of the conspicuous failings of mankind."
> —**Walter Bagehot**

As I have been writing this book, I go to court, and every time I do, I try out my advice on my fellow criminal defense lawyers. I ask them the same question: "If someone is stopped at night by the police for something minor such as not signaling a turn or a lane change, identifies themselves, makes no statements or admissions about drinking, takes no field sobriety tests, and no breath tests on the street, gets arrested, and does not take the station house breath test or blood tests, what does the prosecution have for a DUI case?" So far the answer of my colleagues has been a unanimous and brief **"nothing, no case"**.

So why does the fear of arrest cause running of your mouth which results in your arrest? Why is getting arrested so fear inducing? When compared with certain conviction, an arrest is a short-lived inconvenience. What happens routinely in third world countries that we all hear about or see on television or on film does not happen here. You don't get beaten, locked up in a cell indefinitely and forgotten, have hard, dangerous serial killers for cellmates, or anything of that nature. If you quietly and respectfully submit to arrest, you don't get shocked with a Taser gun, you don't get pepper sprayed, and you don't get beat up. You get handcuffed, searched and taken before a neutral official who may be called a magistrate, justice of the peace, judicial officer, or judge, before whom the arresting officer must state under oath what you did. This is but a momentary inconvenience when compared to what happens if you don't remain silent. Saying anything quickly lapses into saying and doing everything to convict you, and upon conviction you are in the system for a minimum of one year with all manner of government strings attached. I'm not suggesting a win in court is guaranteed if you remain silent. I'm guaranteeing your conviction in court, however, if you do the opposite on the street; open your mouth, and say any more than "I am remaining silent and demand a lawyer".

When you are stopped at night and driving under the influence is suspected by the officer, it is important to remember that it is the officer who has the initiative, by stopping you. His objective is to get you to say and do as much as possible to get the evidence from you he doesn't otherwise have. He will try his best to keep you in a non-custodial state, as long as possible, because as long as you are not in custody, no police recital of *Miranda* warnings is required. But again, you don't need *Miranda* if you remember the Fifth Amendment, your absolute right to say nothing once you identify yourself.

Your objective should be the opposite—to shorten the time you are not in custody. You can accomplish your objective by taking the initiative away from the officer by immediately asking if you are free to leave. He must answer yes or no. If he doesn't answer, keep asking until he does; or start to leave, and tell him this is what you're doing. You will promptly get your answer. When you take the initiative as suggested, and show him you know your rights, you often find, according to client feedback, an officer who doesn't know how to deal with such people. As likely as not, the officer will either not want to bother with people like you and send you on your way, or he will promptly lose patience with you and promptly place you under arrest. This is what you want because arrest neutralizes his advantage over you. He expects you to be intimidated and make verbal mistakes, hoping you will want to avoid being arrested. Most of the people he contacts, in large part because of media misinformation, are predictably scared, and only hurt themselves, mistakenly thinking that talking and testing is required, and will result in being let go. Talking and testing in this situation is most assuredly not required, rarely helps, and in almost all cases, results in arrest and only hurts you later on in court. When you take the initiative, politely, calmly, but firmly, from knowledge of and exercising your rights, you limit his alternatives to two choices; he either lets you go or takes you into custody, and to the judicial officer.

At this point, when you demand a lawyer, and you should use the word "demand", it is the officer that has to shut up or at least stop questioning you, or he himself is breaking the law.

For those who persist in thinking that the arrest matters, if you're not convicted, Virginia and most other jurisdictions have procedures in place to expunge any part of your record. Expungement is a separate legal proceeding which you can do with or without a lawyer, but like most procedures in the legal system, if you want it done right the first time, hire a lawyer.

Yet another example of the love affair of the police with intimidation to get you to talk is to use official sounding words and phrases to suggest legality, legal necessity, scientific validity, and what is required of you to create a sense of compulsion—you must do this or you must do that; you must answer, you must take breath tests, you must take field sobriety tests. This is bullshit! All you must do is identify yourself, and exit your vehicle if told to do so. That's it. These lies, seemingly from mere repetition have become truth according to the police. They believe their own nonsense! No matter how often they are repeated, lies remain lies. You don't have to do anything except identify yourself, and peaceably submit to arrest. The faster you do these things, the better it is for you later on, when you consult a lawyer and thereafter in court. **Your lawyer will love your case.**

PART IV

LEVELING THE PLAYING FIELD

"Never miss a good chance to shut up."
—**Will Rogers**

"It is more noble by silence to avoid injury than by argument to overcome it."
—**Francis Beaumont**

The approach I recommend to avoid conviction is counter-intuitive, doing the opposite of what you might think or were taught or conditioned to think is the right thing or the required thing to do. The approach is what you never would have thought would be most beneficial.

What I say next is not the advice you expected. If you are not free to leave, getting arrested ASAP is the best way to handle a police encounter. It is counter-intuitive and relatively unpleasant, but it is your best move for the best chance to win in court. Why? Because the universal and unwarranted fear of an officer arresting you is their number one tool to get you to screw yourself by talking to them. If you run your mouth, take and fail tests, and admit to an offense, do you really think you will not be arrested? Get real! Saying and doing anything else other than identifying yourself and then telling them you have nothing else to say not only gets you arrested, it dooms your case.

Since adding to my TV diet regular helpings of law and order shows, from the resulting indigestion I decided to push back and do what I could to counter the rampant deception and false information the viewing public receives. I developed a business card with advice you need to have when stopped by the police.

Everything on this card is based on the express language of the Bill of Rights in the Constitution or a decision of the United States Supreme Court, and is therefore the law in all fifty states.

This card was composed and revised over the past ten years with suggestions of colleagues, and after years of frustration from not being able to overcome my clients' mistakes, because they didn't have beforehand the information on this card. My clients almost uniformly react to reading it in my office with

Know and Exercise Your Rights:

BEFORE THE MIRANDA WARNINGS, YOU LAWFULLY CAN AND SHOULD:

➤ If approached by a police officer, ask if you are free to leave; **if yes, walk away immediately. If approached at home, stay inside.**

➤ Refuse to answer all questions except about your identity.

➤ Refuse to consent to any search, or home entry, unless shown a warrant.

➤ Refuse to admit to anything or to explain anything.

➤ Refuse to take any sobriety or other tests or give any evidence.

➤ Demand to have a lawyer present when questioned.

IF STOPPED BY POLICE, BEFORE ANY ARREST:

➤ **DO:** Be calm, polite, and keep your hands visible at all times.

➤ **DO:** Identify yourself fully and agree to come to court.

➤ **DO:** Tell the officer you will talk only about your identity and a court date without a lawyer present. Exit your vehicle if directed to do so.

➤ **DO NOT:** Admit to anything, explain anything, or consent to any search.

➤ **DO NOT:** Take any sobriety test or other tests anywhere.

➤ **DO NOT:** Answer any questions except about your identity.

➤ **DO NOT:** Believe any statement that you will "help" yourself if you "cooperate". Cooperating means giving up these rights and only helps the police by giving them evidence they will use against you. **Cooperation will cause your conviction.**

IF ARRESTED:

➤ **DO NOT RESIST:** You will be handcuffed, searched and promptly taken to a Judicial Officer for bond. Identify yourself and agree to come to Court.

Say nothing else and call a lawyer Immediately.

statements such as "I wish I knew this before I ran into the officer, before I was stopped, before I was arrested". Or, they say, "I didn't know that, I thought I had to cooperate, or it would be better for me if I did." or "I thought I had to take those sobriety tests". In short, an unawareness of their rights.

Over the years since I developed and began handing out this card, clients have reported interesting and amusing (to me) police reactions indicating the effectiveness of its advice when followed. For example, a young man in his mid-twenties was stopped by the police and after providing his license and registration, was asked by the officer, "Have you been drinking tonight?" The response was "I'm not answering, according to my lawyer, I don't have to, it says so on this card", showing it to the officer. He sternly took the card, read it for a moment, tore it to pieces, and threw them on the ground. Handing back the license and registration to the driver, the officer said the card was "bullshit", and told my client to get lost, letting him go without further delay.

The same thing happened to one of my nieces in New Jersey. She was stopped late at night in her home town where, she reports, the police stop young ladies routinely at night on the grounds of "blonde and pretty". The officer, after obtaining her license, said to her "Where are you coming from?" She answered, "I don't have to tell you that". The officer replied, "You have to answer any question I ask you". She then said, "No I don't according to my lawyer; it says so on his card", handing it to the officer. Like the Virginia officer, he read it, tore it up, then said to her as he returned her license, "Go home young lady," ending the encounter.

The police hate this advice because they believe every one they stop to be guilty, know this approach is effective, and they particularly resent young people who indicate they know their rights by showing that they do, and don't give the police what they want. The police are nothing more than government employees with the power to arrest and their authority and enforcement tools often go to their head.

The purpose of the card is inspired by my father, who was a physician from the old school. He was what was called before the age of specialization, a general practitioner. His constant advice was "The best medicine is prevention." The good doctor was an advocate of the basics; regular exercise, a good night's sleep, a balanced diet, and plenty of soap and water, as being the keys to good health. Practicing prevention this way was all that was needed. The same is true for your legal health. The basis of your legal health is preventing the police from getting evidence from you by not giving it to them. In my view there are only four exceptions to remaining silent and saying nothing when you encounter the police. After immediately identifying yourself:

First, ask "Am I free to leave?",

Second, "I am remaining silent and not taking any tests.",

Third, "I demand to talk to a lawyer now.",

Fourth, "Take me to the magistrate now, or let me leave, I have nothing else to say".

> *"He who knows does not speak,*
> *he who speaks does not know."*
> —**Lao Tzu**, Chinese Philosopher 604-531 BC

According to the U.S. Supreme Court, the law requires that a police officer, upon arresting you, bring you without delay to a judicial officer before whom the police officer must state under oath what you did to cause your arrest. The judicial officer will prepare a warrant or summons charging you with an offense based on what the officer said under oath, and then evaluate your likelihood of appearing in court, fix a bond, and in a great majority of misdemeanor offenses, like DUI and marijuana possession, release you on your written promise to appear. In most cases, this entire process takes only a few hours.

Always keep in mind that your silence or choice to advise the officer you do not intend to answer any questions except about your identity, does not furnish grounds to arrest you or detain you. The approach of an officer and your engaging with him is viewed by the law as a consensual encounter, as long as you consent to talk to the officer. You are free to walk away from this encounter at any time, and doing so is not grounds to arrest or detain you, either.

The most serious traffic offense stops are going to get you arrested anyway, so why say or do anything to give the officer the evidence to justify that arrest. Say nothing except discuss a court date, which most officers have assigned monthly and these dates are known by him three or four months in advance. When the officer brings you before the judicial officer, that individual will ask the police officer what you did and what you said. Assuming the arresting officer will tell the judicial officer the truth about what you said—you identified yourself and agreed to come to court—the judicial officer will release you on your written promise to appear in court on the day he tells you, if the magistrate agrees with the officer that you violated the law. That date will be one of the officer's court dates. If you are obviously drunk, the judicial officer will keep you in custody until you sober up, a matter of hours, and then release you.

Suppose the judicial officer does not release you? What then? In Virginia, and most other jurisdictions, the law directs that the person arrested and held in custody appear in court the next business day of the court, where that judge, a trial judge, advises you of the charge, and determines whether you will hire counsel or qualify for a court-appointed attorney, reconsiders the judicial officer's bond decision, and schedules a trial date.

To be held in custody is a rare occurrence in misdemeanor offenses, including serious traffic offenses, such as a DUI. There are not enough jails to hold the number of people charged with these types of offenses pending trial, and so a hierarchy has been created by courts, and by statutes. Nonviolent, victimless misdemeanants commonly get released on bond.

During these uncommon and short detentions, it is highly doubtful that you will be asked questions about the facts of your case. It is during this time you should and will be permitted to make contact with family, lawyers, and a bondsman. Usually, however, including DUI cases, you will be released on a personal promise bond, after a short period when, in the judicial officer's opinion, he thinks any alcohol in your system is not enough to be a risk to yourself or others, usually about four to six hours. The important point to remember is, you are no longer under the pressure of feeling intimidated by the fear of being arrested or by reason of being isolated with the officer and there should be no compulsion to speak about the charge, so don't, until you speak to a lawyer, preferably in his office.

In minor traffic offense situations, once the ticket is issued, you sign it, agreeing to come to court and the officer returns your license and whatever other credentials you gave him, you are free to leave. Sometimes however, particularly with young adults who fit a manufactured "profile", the officer will continue the detention by perhaps asking you if you have any drugs in your car or may he search the car. The answer to both questions should be a firm **no**! Even if you think there's nothing in the vehicle and are tempted to consent to its search, you can never be sure what a passenger or another driver may have left in the car, even if by accident days or weeks earlier. You never have to consent to any search unless you are shown a search warrant, which an officer making a routine traffic stop is highly unlikely to have. Do not consent to such searches because you are not required to. There are only two instances when you must permit the officer to search; if he has and shows you a search warrant or if he arrests you.

If you are foolish enough to consent to a search of your vehicle, during or immediately following a routine traffic stop, you can be sure the officer will thoroughly go into hidden places, trashing your car; and if he finds something illegal such as a forgotten roach, pill bottle, or empty beer can, none of which you were aware of, you can be certain he will then ask you about what he found. Again, you should tell the officer you have nothing to say. Giving any other answer will only result in more questions and it seems over the years that I've been practicing, once the door is opened by that first answer, people seem to think they will help themselves by talking more. This is **the** big mistake. Saying nothing is always the right course, because in Virginia and many other jurisdictions, ownership or occupancy of a vehicle does not, without "more", constitute sufficient proof of possession of what is found in it, especially if the item was found in a hidden place such as under the vehicle seat. The "more" is what you say to the officer. Possession is usually "knowing possession". Show the officer you know nothing — say nothing!

> *"Even a fool when he holdeth his peace, is counted wise."*
> **—Proverbs 17:28**

Turning now to more serious traffic stop situations—drunk driving roadblocks or checkpoints, late night traffic stops, usually conducted by specially trained officers making DUI stops, aggressive or reckless driving stops and like situations; an arrest is much more likely than you getting a summons, ticket or citation. With increasing frequency, particularly around major holidays, police departments set up roadside checkpoints, where everyone must stop briefly for a few questions focused on whether or not the driver has been drinking.

These checkpoints are usually set up on a well-traveled road where visibility is good both for the approaching drivers and the police officers who work these locations. Therefore, do not try to avoid these checkpoints. If you do, and are seen by an officer turning off into an intervening intersection or driveway, they will come after you. It is far better to proceed to the checkpoint normally, because at these checkpoints they haven't seen any questionable driving behavior, unlike the officer who is on patrol, follows you, and has a good opportunity to pick out those minor imperfections they usually use as the excuse to pull you over.

The officer at the checkpoint usually hasn't seen any driving conduct and uses only the "odor of alcohol" or your "bloodshot eyes" as evidence provided you have followed the **Big Four** and haven't given any additional evidence by speaking or testing. If the only evidence they obtain at the checkpoint is an odor of alcohol, that alone is not sufficient for probable cause for a DUI arrest. To an officer, that doesn't matter. That odor may get you arrested when combined with your "being uncooperative" by exercising your rights. That arrest won't amount to much more once that case gets to a lawyer and to court.

These checkpoints are tightly and strictly regulated because they intrude on our right that is guaranteed by the Constitution to be free from general searches. General searches are those lacking in objective probable cause (factual basis). Therefore, in addition to a weak case factually, if you observe the **Big Four** and don't give any verbal or test evidence against yourself, most experienced DUI lawyers can easily mount a legal defense, as well, to the checkpoint because more often than not the police do not comply with the very strict rules governing them. Any discretionary departure from the setup and rules for conducting it is fatal to the evidence gathered from it. Evidence obtained from an illegally set-up or administered checkpoint is deemed evidence from a general search. Evidence from a general search is unconstitutional. Translation: You win! So again, help your lawyer help you, shut up! You'll get what you paid for; a good result.

Typically the officer approaches the stopped driver and may begin by asking the following initial questions: "Do you know why I stopped you?" or, "Have you had anything to drink tonight?" You should have your license out and keep both hands visible and in response to those questions, say only, "Here is my license", and hand it to the officer. Do not answer or say anything else. Don't volunteer any information. The officer will probably repeat the questions and you should reply, "Here's my identification. I have nothing else to say". Whether angered or not, the officer will probably ask you to exit the vehicle. Politely and promptly comply so that he is not required to physically remove you from the car. Do not argue or resist and ask if you are free to leave. If, in the unlikely event he says you may leave, get your license back and do so immediately.

In the more likely event that the officer says, "No, you can't leave", you are under arrest at that point whether or not the officer uses the word arrest. He doesn't have to say that word; as long as you have submitted to his authority and your freedom to leave is restricted verbally or physically by the officer or he has your license in his possession. You are under arrest. Even if you are not handcuffed at that point, you're under arrest if he says you must remain and cannot leave.

What then will happen? If he senses you've been drinking, he probably will ask you again about that subject. Your reply should be, "I choose to say nothing except about my identity and a court date". At this point the officer, convinced you've been drinking, will ask or direct you to perform field sobriety tests and/or give a breath sample by having you blow into a handheld device which the officer will hold in front of you. He may even tell you that you must take these tests. **No you don't.** You do not have to take any test. Again, politely and clearly say no to participate in any such tests. Even if you have had nothing to drink, don't blow! Sugar-free candy or gum chewing may show the same positive result on these devices as a drink containing alcohol. In Virginia, the officer is supposed to tell you that you can refuse to blow into the handheld breath test device without any consequences. Most officers do not tell you that.

At this point, having said no to tests and admitting nothing, if you haven't thoroughly pissed off the officer, he may try the "nice guy" approach and urge you to "cooperate". Don't fall for that. Cooperating with the officer is the same as working with your opponent; the officer is now your opponent and helping him to prosecute and convict you is insane. Why would any rational person cooperate with their opponent in such a situation. Worse yet, cooperating with the officer means giving him evidence he otherwise wouldn't have. You are the only source of most of that evidence, and you hurt your lawyer's ability to help you. Your lawyer, no matter how skilled or experienced, can't make evidence go away; he can't prevent the officer from writing down what you said and did in his notes and reviewing those notes before testifying against you. On the other hand, he can't write down what you'd didn't say, or didn't do. That sort of a lie is too much for most officers.

Don't help the officer cripple your lawyer by running your mouth. You have the absolute Fifth Amendment right not to talk, so **don't**! To those who would say that I'm contradicting myself, the police lie, therefore even if I said nothing, he'd lie about that, my answer is, I don't think so. Shading what you did say or do by his word choice is quite different from making things up that you didn't say or didn't do. That's a line most officers will not cross.

> *"Silence is the true friend that never betrays."*
> **—Confucius**

I reject the notion that people can't follow any instruction, or remember what to do when under the stress of a police encounter and have had a drink or two. Nonsense. These are the steps. After identifying yourself:

1. **Am I free to leave?**,
2. **I am remaining silent and not taking any tests**,
3. **I demand to talk to a lawyer now**,
4. **Take me to the magistrate now or let me leave.**

Notice throughout, that when you are referring to wanting to talk to a lawyer, I use the word "demand". This is the word that you should use, according to the most recent decision of the United States Supreme Court on this subject. This court, and most other lower appeals courts, State and Federal, are chipping away and narrowing the circumstances when *Miranda* applies to you. The current thinking is that you must clearly demand to consult with a lawyer.

The U.S. Supreme Court also ruled in 2013 that the act of remaining silent alone, without **affirmatively** mentioning or referring to the content of the Fifth Amendment is not sufficient. You now **must verbalize** that you are choosing not to talk and then be quiet. You must now use words when indicating to the police you are choosing not to speak or are remaining silent. Mere silence is not enough, as mere silence is conduct, not speech, and conduct, though not proof of much, can be used against you and commented upon by a prosecutor.

Yet another favored approach of the police is to appeal to your good judgment or intelligence and goes something like, "you're not helping yourself by not talking" or "be sensible" or "help us understand the situation". Giving into and believing such statements is like believing anything they tell you, the worst judgment imaginable. You wouldn't accept medical advice from an accountant. Why take legal advice from anyone but a lawyer, particularly not from a police officer who has stopped you? You only demonstrate intelligence when you don't believe them when they say such nonsense. Remember, when they're talking to you, they want evidence from you they don't yet have. You should immediately after hearing such statements ask if you are free to leave even if you have already done so and have not gotten an answer. At some point, the officer is going to answer yes, or no. If he doesn't answer, you can obtain the answer from him by walking or driving away even if he has your license. Only a foolish officer would charge you with operating a vehicle without your license that was in his possession because he asked for and got it from you. If he stops you physically or verbally, you'll have your answer. You're under arrest. You should at that point, having read this far, know exactly what to do.

If you don't get a prompt answer to "Am I free to leave?", you might try the flip side of that question; "Am I under arrest?" Most officers will answer that question with "No", because if they say "Yes", they must then recite the *Miranda* warning if they want to then question you, and if you heed the warning, they won't be able to get evidence from you. The answer from the officer to either question establishes your custody status and is good for you because whatever he answers, you are either free to leave or in custody, and he then must take you to the judicial officer without delay.

When before the judicial officer, talk to him or her only about such things as your identity, bond, a court date, and nothing else. Your identity may include where you live or work, your marital status, any dependent children, relatives in the nearby area, and if you have ever failed to appear in court before. All of these things are factors in the judicial officer's bond determination. You should freely discuss these matters with the judicial officer, but not the offense or the facts which brings you before him. Usually they stay away from that subject; so should you.

Some officers, who regard themselves as clever, will attempt to create a "gray" area as to your arrest status by inconsistent signals, such as applying a physical restraint or a show of authority, accompanied by verbally telling you the opposite; that you are not under arrest. You must, as quickly as possible, get clarification of whether you are free to go, or not. Keep asking until you get an answer, "Am my free to leave?" or, "Am I under arrest?" Otherwise, in this "gray" period of time, the police will be attempting to get evidence from you because many judges will conclude you are not under arrest and when you are not under arrest the officer is not required to take you to the magistrate, nor is he required to recite the *Miranda* warnings, which you shouldn't need to hear if you just shut up. Asking if you are free to leave or under arrest should be the only topic you take up with them until you get an answer.

A considerable number of clients, when asked by me why they spoke, will say something like, "I told them the truth about what I had to drink because I didn't want to lie". My response is and always will be, you don't have to lie; simply don't answer. Tell the officer you have nothing to say, "I choose to remain silent", using those exact words. You can't lie when you don't talk and you remain silent. If you use these exact words, "I'm sorry officer, I am remaining silent.", the officer should recognize that you are mindful of your Fifth Amendment right to silence and will probably give up trying to get you to talk, and just arrest you.

Another verbal approach the police like to use is to tell you to take or accept responsibility for your conduct. A variation of this approach is "do what is right" or, "do the right thing". The police have a peculiar view of what is right and what is responsible. To the police, it is their code for you to confess and relieve them of the burden of proving your guilt the hard way. My view of accepting responsibility is the acceptance of punishment after the state has proven your guilt by the rules and without your help. To me, taking responsibility does not mean, like it does to the police, that you confess, and help the government convict you. That view of the police on taking responsibility—help them convict you—pure rubbish.

Also employed by the police are the following two approaches, particularly after you advise them you're not talking: "If you don't answer, you are resisting arrest, obstructing justice" or, "You're breaking the law". Each of these is more nonsense. This is lying in its most offensive form. You are not breaking the law when you are exercising your right to silence. Words or silence alone, do not constitute obstructing justice, or resisting arrest. Both of these offenses require physical interference with the officer, something very rarely justified, useful, or safe.

One of my favorite lines used by the police is, "Do you want to go to jail?" Shock the officer; answer, "Yes, let's go to the magistrate right now". In reply, they may tell you jail is a terrible place where bad things happen. The truth is, in the unlikely event the judicial officer does not release you, having given the police officer nothing to tell the judicial officer, you are not jailed very long, and you're usually held, during these brief stays in a holding or booking area, not in a general jail population. Jailing you is a magistrate's or judges' decision, not the officer's, and is very unlikely in traffic or misdemeanor cases.

> *"Silence is the universal refuge."*
> **—Henry David Thoreau**

After traffic stops, police encounters at home are, in my experience, the next most likely place to have face to face dealings with a police officer. The same advice applies to these encounters when it comes to talking, explaining, or answering police questions. Unlike your automobile though, you have greater Constitutional protection against government intrusion in your home or residence; broader and more closely guarded by the courts. In American law the home is sacred.

Suppose, while you, as a parent, are away and your college age kids and their friends throw a party in your home and an uninvited neighbor resents not being invited, thinks the music is too loud or alcohol is being consumed or marijuana smoked, and he calls the police. One or more officers show up at the front door, knock, and your son or daughter who's hosting the party answers the door. What should be done? First, in the unlikely event the officer at the door has a search or arrest warrant, this is the **only** circumstance you must allow him entry. Before doing so, however, you should ask to see the warrant. If they have such written authority to enter, they should and most likely will promptly let you see it. If they tell you they don't have a warrant, they may not enter without your consent. Do not consent, or invite them in. You should remain inside. It is your Constitutional right to keep them out unless they have a warrant. Why not let the police inside? They can see what is in plain view once inside your home, and if it is illegal, they can seize it and arrest you. If they acquire enough information to arrest someone while they are inside, they can search the area within the reach of the person arrested without a search warrant. When that happens they usually exceed the legally permissible area of where they can search, and do the same thing to your home as to your car; they trash the place and you have little or no recourse. Just like in the case of traffic stops, at home, you have an absolute right not to answer questions or say anything. If they don't have either a search or arrest warrant, you can refuse to open the door and ignore them. If they force their way in, without such written authority, they've got problems.

If they have an arrest warrant, and the person named in the warrant is inside, that person should submit to arrest by stepping outside where the police should remain. The officer may try to escort you back in to get your identification. Make sure it is on you when you step outside, and submit to the arrest, otherwise the officer must go with you inside because you are in his custody, and he may see and then can seize, anything unlawful that is in plain view. Another alternative is to try to avoid this entry by the officer by going with him to the judicial officer and try to call someone to bring your identification to you. If at all possible, do not allow the officer inside, if you are arrested outside. This limits the ability of the officers to search inside the home when the arrest is outside. Once you are arrested and identify yourself, you should remain silent until taken to the judicial officer and then only discuss your identity, matters concerning bond, and a court date. Make sure you say nothing else to the judicial officer if the arresting officer is within hearing range. In Virginia, the judicial officer can't be a witness against you in any court proceeding, but if the arresting officer hears what you say to the judicial officer, the arresting officer can testify to what he heard. The objective here is, like in traffic stops, not to give them evidence by talking. The point to always remember is that in all circumstances, at all times, you have a Constitutional right to remain silent whether or not you are told as part of the *Miranda* warning. You can't say the wrong thing when you say nothing.

Don't even speak on the subject to a friend, parent, brother, sister or anyone, because they can be compelled to testify against you if they heard damaging admissions from you that the police know about. Don't use the phone to call any of these people, even to a spouse, from a police station telephone, except to discuss arranging bond. These calls are monitored by the police, except and only except when you are on the phone with your lawyer. In that event, you should specifically say so at the start of this call, and even then you should be guarded in what you say until you are in the privacy of your lawyer's office. If the police eavesdrop on such a call to your lawyer, they are committing the felony of wiretapping without legal authority, and invading the attorney/client privilege.

If the police do enter a residence, and see, for example, what looks to them to be marijuana on a coffee table, or alcoholic beverage containers in open view and people appearing under the legal drinking age in the same room, that alone is not enough to get anyone in trouble. A currently popular pretext of the police to gain entry without a warrant is to claim they smell marijuana, even if they don't. If they do smell marijuana, in fact, don't panic. The police, in order to make a case, must connect what they see in the open to a person. Merely being present, and in the same room, provided you say nothing, is not enough to connect anyone present to any pot or alcohol the officer may observe, nor is it sufficient to make a case in court, and the police know it, even though they will act and speak to the contrary. This is the time to remember to remain silent. Only your talking, at this point, connects you to the alcohol or pot, if any is seen.

Their investigation will proceed with the standard battery of lies earlier discussed to try to get you to make the necessary connection for them between you and the pot or the alcohol they observed. Only you can make the connection for them by opening your mouth. Keep it shut, even if someone else points the finger at you. You are not required to answer, cooperate, tell your side, follow their recommendations or advice, or accept their opinions. Your only obligation is to yourself. With clarity and certainty, tell them you have nothing to say. When doing so, you must leave no doubt or ambiguity in asserting the right to remain silent, to have a lawyer, and not engage in any further communication with the police. The police are keenly aware of their helplessness when you choose to remain silent and demand a lawyer, and they will go to great lengths, including threats (to arrest everyone present unless someone claims the pot or the alcohol as theirs), deception, as well as wrong advice, to get you to talk and claim the alcohol or pot as yours. Don't respond. Call their bluff if they threaten to arrest all present. Answer with, "Okay, let's all go to the magistrate right now". Your lawyer will make short work of any charge brought in these circumstances, provided you and everyone else say nothing more.

Does giving the police the "silent treatment" piss them off? Probably. Does that make things worse for you? Absolutely not! They want you to think otherwise, that silence is unwise, or even illegal. Silence is neither. You must keep in mind what's good for your case when it gets to court and not worry about what happens in the next couple of minutes or hours after that first encounter. Your mindset should be the same as the officer's only in one respect. When he's dealing with you, he's preparing a case against you for court. You should also be preparing your case for court by remaining silent. He's gathering his most effective evidence against you from you; you should stop him with the most effective tool you have, your silence. His leverage to get you to speak is the threat of arrest. Your leverage not to speak is the Constitutional right to silence. You will gain nothing as far as not being arrested is concerned by talking and testing. You will be arrested, with no chance in court, and convicted. Just remember your main objective—your bottom line—is not to be convicted in court; to win!

> *"Most wrongdoing works, on the whole, less mischief than its useless confession."*
> —**Edith Wharton**

To effectively communicate your intention to remain silent and to consult counsel, you must leave no doubt or ambiguity. You must not leave any room for someone else's judgment or discretion as to what you intend and demand. Wording such as: "I might want a lawyer", "Should I have a lawyer", "Do I need an attorney", "Do you think I need an attorney here with me", or "You did say I could have an attorney if I wanted" are **all** inadequate! The police are not required to get clarification or an interpretation of what you meant and if you need to clarify what you mean or demand, you are not doing it right. To leave no doubt, you must use the magic words! They are few in number, and easy to remember: "I have nothing to say", "I am remaining silent", "I demand to see a lawyer". Believe it or not, libraries of law books are filled with decisions analyzing what were insufficient invocations of the right to silence and counsel. There are a bewildering number of court decisions interpreting the equal bewildering variety of word combinations human speech utilizes to express what one means or intends. Simplicity of word choice and sticking to that choice is the only safe insurance against the police persisting in talking to you to get you to give them evidence, or a judge ruling that you didn't make yourself clear. If you keep it simple, they should get the message, and leave you alone. Remember, they are not accustomed to dealing with people who know their rights and often give up when they encounter such people and do the only thing they know at that point; they disengage from you or become irritated and arrest you. That's all they've got when you've made it simple for them—**I am not talking!**

Here's how to do it right, after identifying yourself:

1. **Am I a free to leave? (If yes, skip 2–4, and leave! If no, proceed as follows.),**
2. **I'm remaining silent and not taking any tests,**
3. **I demand to speak to a lawyer now,**
4. **I have nothing else to say.**

Use the fewest words possible to get your message across. The more words used, the more wiggle room there is for the police to distort what you said or meant, for the prosecutor to argue you meant something else, weren't sure what you wanted, weren't clear to the police who therefore, continued to press you to talk, or you waived your right to remain silent and have a lawyer present. Be especially careful not to engage in any conversation no matter how innocent or seemingly unrelated to your arrest. Such conversations put you at risk for a slip of the tongue, say to the police that you waive your right to silence, and/or are willing to talk. You can't make a mistake if you don't talk.

Most importantly, doing it right includes style and manner of delivering your message. When communicating with the officer in the limited way advised, make sure your tone in getting your message across, is not confrontational, not arrogant, not belligerent in any way. No "I'll show you" attitude. You should sound apologetic. For example, "I'm sorry officer, I'm remaining silent", or "I don't mean to be difficult officer, but I'm not taking any test", or "Sorry sir (ma'am) you may not search unless you have a warrant". For the most part in urban areas officers are disciplined professionals, and should respect your choices. No matter what the officer then says and does, **don't change your mind**. Go with the flow and stay focused on your objective—winning in court.

In misdemeanor cases and particularly in DUI and marijuana cases, where the press and the public exert great pressure on the legal system to be "tough on crime", it is next to impossible to suppress (keep out of evidence) and keep the judge from considering statements made by you which are damaging. As noted previously, the law in this area is extensive, highly fact specific, and its application to your specific set of facts makes predicting the outcome of these motions exceedingly difficult. Suppression is not a popular remedy, judges know it, don't like to suppress evidence, and such motions are rarely successful. Therefore, the safest and smartest thing to do is to avoid such issues, legal debates, and the need for your lawyer to file and argue such motions, so as not to expose your case to a potential legal mistake or ruling against you by the court, is to not make statements to the police in the first place. There can be no legal dispute or legal debate, and nothing to decide incorrectly, nor doubt about what you said, if you have said nothing. The judge can't hear incriminating statements never spoken—statements that don't exist. There are, thankfully, few officers that would make up a confession not actually made.

> *"You don't have to explain something you never said."*
> —**Calvin Coolidge**

To illustrate how the police can distort what you say, I'm reminded of the famous scene in the movie "My Cousin Vinnie" where the sheriff wrote down a purported confession to a murder, which was, in fact the opposite. The sheriff was interrogating young Mr. Gambini about the facts of a murder of a store clerk. Mr. Gambini assumed he was being questioned about a can of tuna he didn't pay for at the store where the clerk was shot. At the point where the sheriff said "and then you shot the clerk", Gambini replied "I shot the clerk?" in his typical New York style. The sheriff, from the Deep South, was obviously not accustomed to dealing with northerners and how they speak; in his notes of the conversation, he wrote that Gambini said "I shot the clerk", minus the question mark and testified to this "confession" in court.

I defended a rape case where a similar distortion occurred by a civilian acting as an auxiliary police officer who served as a Spanish interpreter for the police. Currently, many officers are bilingual, particularly in Spanish. This auxiliary officer was used to interrogate my client who was an immigrant from Latin America and who spoke no English. My client was apprehended by accident while he and several of his companions was actually engaged in sexual intercourse on the open ground of a public park at night. The apprehension occurred because a police helicopter was searching the ground by spotlight from overhead. The helicopter had been dispatched to the park to search for a fleeing suspect who had just robbed a business next to the park, completely unrelated to the rape incident. As the searchlight was panning the ground, in search of the robber, who was last seen running into the park, my client was seen actually in the act of intercourse, on the ground, with a woman.

He and his companions had been with the alleged victim of the rape the preceding 6-8 hours drinking and dancing with the victim in a Mexican restaurant also close to the park. The victim was drunk, and we were also able to discover that she had made two previous false charges of sexual assault and she admitted she had just separated from her husband and was soliciting money at the bar from my client as well as other patrons, citing that she had no place to stay. When the helicopter reported the observation of the sexual activity on the ground to officers on routine patrol near the park, those officers went into the park and apprehended my client, still engaged in intercourse, with the woman. Upon separating them, the victim never stated to the officers initially that she had been raped, but claimed she was a short time later.

When my client was taken to the police station to be interrogated, the civilian auxiliary officer, serving as the interpreter for the police, recorded in his written (not audio recorded) notes that my client said, "**Yes**, I raped her I ought to go to jail". When I interviewed my client in jail, he said to me that he told the interpreter, "**If**, I raped her I ought to go to jail", and that she consented.

At trial, on cross-examination, the interpreter admitted that the Spanish word for "if" and "yes" is identical—"si". On the basis of the victim's prior false complaints of rape and my client's testimony that he told the interpreter, "**If I raped her . . .** " reasonable doubt was created on the issue of consent and the defendant was acquitted by the jury of the charge.

The lesson here—a distortion is potentially deadly and can happen easily. If this interpreter was told nothing by the defendant, except "I choose to remain silent, and demand a lawyer immediately", no distortion or a misinterpretation would have occurred, as the risk of that happening would have been eliminated by the defendant's silence and the relatively weak case of the prosecution.

It can't be overstated, or too often repeated, how heavily dependent the police and the government are on your ignorance of, and thereby giving up, your right to remain silent. In the final analysis, the short term inconvenience and temporary embarrassment of getting arrested is indeed a small price to pay for a better than 50/50 chance of avoiding a criminal conviction by not talking to the police or taking any of their tests. The government's conviction rate, their batting average of ninety percent plus, drops dramatically without your talking or testing.

Recent feedback to me from clients who have shown the police they know their rights, has indicated that the police, as often as not, back off and stop questioning, if you do it right. Don't waste your breath saying things like "I have Constitutional rights" or "I know my rights". Don't tell the officer—show him you know. Just say the magic words.

> *"These words, hereafter, thy tormentors be."*
> **—Shakespeare**
>
> *"The world would be happier if men had the same capacity to be silent that they have to speak".*
> **—Spinoza**

Every day, lawyers debate in court with judges, consuming thousands of hours for what I contend is little more than a waste of time over whether a confession was voluntary, whether the encounter with the officer was and remained consensual, whether any statements were coerced, whether a person's *Miranda* warnings were required, clearly invoked, whether there was an interrogation by the officer, whether there was an arrest, a detention, and on, and on, and on. The point is these endless legal discussions and debates in court, all with the objective of demonstrating the police acted illegally, so as to, in turn, obtain suppression of statements of the defendant, are rarely successful, and would be unnecessary if, during the initial encounter, the person approached by the police simply said nothing before seeing a lawyer.

Yet another method of the police is to say "if you have nothing to hide, or didn't do anything wrong, you would consent" to a search, "talk to us", or "take these tests". This is more bullshit. You should stand firm and not consent. If the officer threatens to arrest you, tell him to go ahead. Do not physically resist, submit to an arrest. Your lawyer can and will deal with that issue, probably successfully, if something illegal is found in your car, provided you have kept your mouth shut when the officer starts asking you about what he found. Hopefully, some form of recording might be made as the police now often use on-board cameras or recorders in their patrol vehicles. If you have verbally objected and by shaking your head to indicate "no" (for the camera), your lawyer will know how to get that recording for use in your favor. Even without any other documentation of the encounter, your denial of consent preserves your lawyer's ability to challenge the correctness of the arrest or search. If you consent, on the other hand, that consent usually forfeits any claim of illegality by which the search took place. **Do not consent to anything except giving your identity and agreeing to appear in court.** Keep in mind that your arrest triggers the officer's ability to search you and your vehicle. No matter what he finds, if anything, and asks you about it, continue to remain silent and state again you want a lawyer present before answering any questions.

If you are pulled over at any time, do you have to exit the vehicle if asked or directed to do so? The U.S. Supreme Court has ruled that you must do so. Officers will ask for safety reasons, but the real reason is to begin observing your coordination, balance, muscle control, and general appearance, as these are all components of the definition of intoxication or being under the influence. These two terms have the identical definition in Virginia.

Consistent with the counter-intuitive approach I advocate and recommend, as soon as you are asked to exit the vehicle you should reply, "Am I free to leave?" The very probable answer will be no, at which point you should step out and tell the officer, "Since I'm not free to leave, put the cuffs on me and take me to the magistrate". The police officer, by placing you in handcuffs, is less able to observe any independent lack of muscle coordination you may exhibit by your exiting the vehicle on your own, such as leaning on the car for balance. His physical contact with you and positioning you to be searched and handcuffed ends voluntary independent movement on your part and compromises his claim that you lacked coordination or muscle control.

Once you have exited the car, if he hasn't already done so, tell him again to place you in handcuffs. Then tell him to immediately take you to the judicial officer, and that you have nothing else to discuss without a lawyer present, and that you will not be taking any test. These are the only and last words that should come out of your mouth until you are in front of a judicial officer. You have now stopped, or at least reduced, his evidence gathering ability. Moreover, when you're ordered from the car, the officer provides strong evidence of the fact of your arrest and coupled with your not making any admissions about alcohol or drug consumption and taking no field or on-the-street breath tests, he has little more than "mere odor" plus the minor traffic infraction, usually having nothing to do with lack of control of the vehicle or its safe operation.

I know of few prosecutors who would be enthusiastic about prosecuting such a weak set of facts as a full blown DUI case. Such a case is ripe for negotiation for a reduced charge, both as to the merits of the DUI and the refusal charge, because of the questionable factual basis for the DUI arrest. Remember, it takes a valid DUI arrest to trigger the implied consent to take the police station breath test, and a valid arrest must be based on objective facts, which the officer will not have if you don't volunteer them, and are promptly cuffed and transported.

The most difficult decision you will have to make after a DUI arrest, but before release by the magistrate, is whether or not to take the station house breath test. You are told that test is required by what is known as "implied consent laws"—by driving on the public highway and provided you are validly arrested for DUI, you have implied your consent to give a sample of your breath at the police station for analysis to see if you are over the legal limit of alcohol in your blood. You may refuse to take this test, but if you do, and you are validly arrested for DUI, you are subject to a separate charge of refusal. In Virginia, you can refuse if the refusal is reasonable or your DUI arrest was lacking in probable cause (legal speak for observed facts). What is reasonable is very narrow and lawyers who are experienced in these cases vary in advising on what to do. In Virginia, the implied consent to take the police station breath test—not to be confused with the handheld breath test device at the stop scene—depends on and requires a valid arrest for DUI. Without a valid arrest, no breath or blood test at the police station is required. That is why it is so important for you to say as little as possible at the scene, and any time thereafter, and take no tests whatsoever. The less you say and do, the more likely it is that your lawyer can demonstrate that your arrest for DUI was lacking in probable cause, and therefore, not a valid arrest. If your lawyer can demonstrate an invalid arrest, both the DUI charge and the refusal charge, based on not taking the station house test, should fail in court.

Don't make the mistake of thinking that if the officer has a basis to pull you over for the usual claim of weaving, or something like failing to use a turn signal that this constitutes probable cause to arrest for DUI. It does not. Such driving is only the basis for stopping you. When you disregard my advice and take tests, make admissions, answer questions, or think he's got you so you might as well tell all after being stopped, this is what is going to give him the factual basis to arrest he otherwise wouldn't have. Once you do that, it's over. Minor defects in your driving are the basis to stop you. The basis to arrest you for DUI is quite different. That basis is usually your big mouth, your inability to close it, and cooperating, by taking the field tests.

Fewer people the police stop are truly intoxicated and all over the road than is generally believed. Most have had a drink or two, but to hear the exaggerated descriptions of your driving conduct, one would think you were in a demolition derby and falling down drunk. In these circumstances, it is rare for an officer on patrol who pulls you over late at night to let you go, if the officer obtains the slightest indication of drinking by you. To begin with, the officer assumes people driving at that hour have been drinking. The officer's mindset is to be looking for these drivers and the smallest driving imperfection stands out, and is usually the officer's rationale for stopping you, because such driving is easily noticed when there are few cars on the road. During daylight hours, these driving imperfections are minor adjustments we all make in response to traffic conditions, but to an officer at night, it is, in his mind, reason to stop you. Suspicion may be a basis to stop you, but what you do and say after you're stopped is the basis to arrest and convict you. If you say and do nothing, the officer has only suspicion or his annoyance at your lack of cooperation on which to base the arrest. His annoyance and suspicion are never a basis for a conviction in court. In my experience, you are probably going to get arrested when stopped late at night. Once again, be quiet and get arrested as soon as possible. Even if it means pissing off the officer, so be it. When he's pissed off, you're doing what you're supposed to do.

DUI cases have become a mainstay of the serious traffic misdemeanor cases on the dockets of most lower courts, especially in metropolitan areas. DUI is a serious matter because irresponsible drinking and driving is a serious social problem and state legislatures annually ratchet up the DUI laws and the severity of the consequences for violating these laws. That doesn't mean that society should combat this problem at the expense of the basic rights of persons accused of this or any offense. The restraints on the power of government that are your Constitutional Rights have historically been a tempting target for government relaxation of those restraints when confronted by serious social problems such as irresponsible drinking and driving, or any crime. I am happy to report that the Constitutional Rights of the accused continue to trump the needs of the government in addressing social problems according to the Supreme Courts of the States and the U.S. Supreme Court. *Miranda*, after nearly half a century of criticism by the police and distortion by the media, is still the law of the land. The only reason, in my opinion, why we don't hear more about the Fifth Amendment is even if people know that it exists, they don't know when to take advantage of it when it matters most. Very few people are taking advantage of these rights, which the high courts continue to uphold in the face of non-stop efforts of the police to evade them.

> *"Little said is soonest mended."*
> **—George Wither**

All of the most persuasive evidence of DUI is within your exclusive control and is only available to the police if you give it to them; something you're not required to do. If you were drinking, how much you drank, what you drank, and when you drank it, how whatever you had to drink affected your behavior, balance, muscle control, coordination, and general appearance are only determinable and observable by the officer if you consent to take field sobriety tests or blow into an alcohol breath test device, answer questions or make voluntary statements. You are not legally required to do any of these things, so don't! Your lawyer can work with and overcome almost any piece of negative evidence, except your statements and test taking.

At night, as soon as the officer mentions the subject—and he probably will—of alcohol, you are most likely going to be arrested no matter what you say or do. If you stand on your rights, you will be arrested because you will be viewed and described by the officer as belligerent or aggressive, a smartass, difficult, or having something to hide, and guilty simply because you exercised your right to silence and didn't take any tests. Alternatively, if you make admissions about alcohol consumption, and take any tests, which are designed for you to fail, and you will fail, you will still get arrested. All you will have accomplished is to give the officer damaging, incriminating detail to tell the prosecutor and the judge and your conviction in court is certain.

If you are not in a large metropolitan area, are arrested on a Friday or Saturday night, and there is no judicial officer on duty, the very worst case scenario is that you'll be before a judge on Monday morning, and held in custody from the time of your arrest until that court appearance—a comparatively small price to pay for a probable victory in court. Moreover, that time in jail is a strong bargaining chip for your lawyer, in a weak case, which will be weak if you don't talk and don't test.

The same approach should be applied if the officer suspects or talks about marijuana. What to watch for here is the request to search your car either before or after a traffic citation is written. Such requests should always be answered with a polite but firm "**No!**". Your refusal to consent is not a basis for the search that the officer asked you to allow him to do. Your choice not to consent to a search of your car will be met by the officer saying, "If you have nothing to hide, you will let me search". You should immediately respond with, "Am I free to leave?" If the officer says, "Yes", get back your ID, and leave immediately. If the officer says, "No, you can't leave", tell him to immediately place you in handcuffs and take you to the judicial officer, and say nothing else. Don't worry about the resulting search of your car following your arrest provided you say nothing. Even if the arrest is lawful, and the search of your car turns up anything illegal, that was not in plain view, (under the passenger seat, for example) if you keep your mouth shut when asked about it, the mere finding of it in your car proves nothing for which you can be successfully prosecuted. If the arrest is illegal, and in the above scenario it probably is, your lawyer will know what to do.

Currently popular with the police is, upon you're not agreeing to let him search your person or your car, is his claiming that he smells marijuana, and tells you that he is going to call for a "sniffer" dog, and you will have to wait for its arrival. If you are compelled to remain until the dog arrives, and you have said nothing up to that point, that waiting period is arguably an illegal detention, so long as you continue to ask if you are free to leave and say nothing else. While awaiting the arrival of the dog, and after he "alerts" on your car, and the dog will, for a small trace of pot you might not even know or recall was in the car, that detention to await the arrival of the dog and the search by the officer will probably be illegal, and whatever was found kept out of evidence in your case by most competent lawyers. Your detention after receiving an answer that you are not free to leave is probably illegal because it is without any supporting objective facts. This is particularly true if you are given a ticket for a traffic infraction and your remaining in the officer's presence is compelled by his refusal to release you after you have signed the ticket, have asked to leave, and said no to his search request.

If you are detained until the dog arrives, remain silent and don't panic, even though these dogs are rarely wrong. The dog will alert on your car if pot is in it, or was recently. Even if the officer finds any pot, and the prosecutor manages to convince the judge the detention and the search was legal, you will still win if you keep your mouth shut, and admit or explain nothing, unless the pot is found on your person, or in plain view within your reach. The officer will probably show you what he found in the vehicle and ask you about it. Tell him you have nothing to say. The mere ownership or occupancy of a vehicle or dwelling where pot or any drug is found is insufficient proof without more for a conviction in most states. Again, the more is your big mouth—shut it!

> *"Silence alone is great, all else is weakness."*
> **—Alfred DeVigney**
>
> *"To use silence in time and place passeth all well speaking."*
> **—Stefano Guazzo**

Once in a great while a lawyer can win your case for some unexpected and infrequent clerical mistake made by the government in which evidence or required paperwork is mishandled, lost, or not filed on time. Reliance on such fortuitous rarities to win is foolish. The only way to consistently win is to consistently remain silent.

In over four and a half decades of criminal trial practice, I've seen only one instance in which physical resistance to a police officer's unlawful arrest was justified. I represented a young, single mother of a three-year-old child, who called 911 from her home, a sixth floor apartment in a mid-rise building in Northern Virginia. In the emergency call, she reported that her child was throwing up uncontrollably, and she didn't know what to do; "Please help." she told the 911 operator. She sounded hysterical on the phone, as the boy was choking on his vomited liquid. Emergency medical help responded along with two uniformed police officers at her front door. She opened the door, holding her child, who was seated on her forearm, just fine, not throwing up, not crying, not doing anything, just sitting on his mother's arm. The emergency personnel asked if she needed any help, and she said she did not, everything was okay now, thanks for responding, and good night.

Both the emergency personnel and the police officers, one male and one female, in uniform, were standing in the hall of the apartment house and my client was inside her apartment. The male officer proceeded to question my client, and after she assured the officers that everything was now okay, the child was fine, no one else was in the apartment, and further police questioning having nothing to do with why she called 911 in the first place, she grew impatient with the questioning officer. She then thanked everyone for responding, and began to close her apartment door. The male officer placed his foot between the door and the door frame to prevent it being closed. He then proceeded to push the door open, reached into the apartment, and forcibly pulled the child out of its mother's arms, handed the child to the EMT personnel who ran with the child down the hall to the elevator, apparently not accepting the mother's word, and seeing for themselves that the child was okay.

The officer placed the mother in handcuffs after pulling her out of her apartment. Upon seeing the EMT personnel running down the hall with the child, she went quite understandably hysterical. The more outraged she became, the more physical restraint was applied by the police, which led to further hysteria by my client and more physical force by the police, who eventually took my client, still in handcuffs, down an elevator to the apartment house lobby where she continued to resist and scream for the return of her child, as well as protest what was happening to her.

At this point, additional officers arrived, and forcibly applied leg restraints around her ankles—handcuffs for the lower legs. Continuing to scream and resist being taken away in the police paddy wagon, having done nothing wrong except protest physically and verbally the forced separation from her child, who was okay, three or four police officers picked her off the ground like a log to throw her into the paddy wagon. The male officer, who forced his way into her apartment, was holding her around the head, in headlock fashion, with her face against his side just above his gun belt.

As the officers were unceremoniously hauling her into the paddy wagon, she used the only weapon left available to her to resist a clearly unlawful arrest. She bit the officer on his side, breaking the skin. This is a felony in Virginia—

assaulting an officer while in the course of his police duties carrying a mandatory minimum jail sentence of six months.

This lady had a solid defense, as the officer who had reached into her apartment, had committed several crimes in doing what he did by entering her apartment without any warrant, without observing any law violation, assaulting her, and abducting her child, without seeing her commit any offense. Because my client wanted to go to trial, but sought from me a guarantee of the outcome, and because she insisted on not going to jail, if she lost at trial—something no lawyer can or should guarantee—a very satisfactory plea bargain was reached with the prosecutor in which the final result was a misdemeanor, with all jail time suspended.

As noted at the outset, these facts were most unusual, and my educated guess is that a jury would probably have found her not guilty, but as in every case, each side has a risk of losing at trial especially in cases such as this. Therefore, a negotiated outcome was probably the best resolution for both sides. Note, however, that the woman did not say the wrong things to the police. These officers were clearly wrong, and overreached their authority. If the officer had simply arrested the woman, without entering her home, grabbing and handing off her child, a judicial officer would most likely not even have issued an arrest warrant and released her. The arresting officer would have been hard pressed on these facts when questioned by the judicial officer as to what the lady did wrong. He would have had little to say.

Again, this was a rare set of circumstances. Do not physically resist being arrested. The officer carries with him too much firepower, not enough judgment, next to zero tolerance for your disagreement with him, or her, and you could get seriously hurt. They have the tools to do it and won't hesitate to use them in a physical fight with you. Verbal objection, particularly if witnesses are present is okay, but that's it! Let your lawyer do the fighting verbally in court, and before that, in the prosecutor's office. Your lawyer will have plenty of leverage if you have kept your mouth shut on the street.

If an officer does not honor your choice to remain silent at any time after you demand a lawyer following arrest, he deserves a written complaint to his Chief of Police. When you clearly tell him you have nothing to say and demand a lawyer, he must honor that choice and stop questioning you. Your choice, to quote the United States Supreme Court in its *Miranda* decision, must be "fully" and "scrupulously" honored.

Under no circumstance, should you ever file a complaint against an officer while your case is pending. After the case is over, in the unusual circumstance of an officer abusing you, a written complaint to the Chief of Police is the proper way to address such abuse, not to the judge. If your complaint is justified and has merit, it will be placed in that officer's file and if he is habitually abusive, he will be properly dealt with internally and hopefully removed from contact with the public. Police Chiefs want to know about such officers, because an abusive officer probably is a dishonest one also. He will dig in his heels if he knows a complaint is filed against him when he testifies against you to justify his conduct. He will either testify falsely or use word choices to put you in the worst possible light, coming as close as he possibly can to lying without actually doing so. In the absolute worst case scenario, he will lie in his defense of your prematurely filed complaint. If you insist on complaining against the officer, save it until the case is over, and don't say to anyone that you plan to do so.

> *"Drawing on my fine command of the English language, I said nothing."*
> **—Robert Benchley**

Don't worry about getting roughed up by the officer; if you have been calm, polite, and not disrespectful, with no belligerent tone, and if you don't physically resist, he will not have to use force. If he does use unnecessary or excessive force and roughness, probably because he was irritated by you not talking and not testing, the officer exposes himself to a complaint to his Chief by you. In a bad case of unnecessary roughness, a criminal assault charge, or better yet, a civil suit for assault. Usually he will tell you to place your hands on a vehicle, his or yours, or behind you, search for weapons on you, immediately after that handcuff you, and transport you to the judicial officer. It's as simple as that. In over forty-eight years both as a prosecutor and defense lawyer, I personally can recall no more than two or three instances where officers went overboard and didn't do their job by the book, as they are trained, and in a calm, business-like professional way. Instances of law enforcement behaving badly do occur, but are much overstated and over dramatized by the media. For every single video recording shown on the evening news of officers behaving badly, the number of routine, professionally executed arrests is in the hundreds of thousands. "Rodney King style" arrests are comparatively rare, and are newsworthy nationally precisely because of their rarity and extreme brutality. Police encounters that end up as shown in movies such as "L.A. Confidential" are from a long bygone time in our country, and as a practical matter, are infrequent today. If you remain calm and cool, most probably the officer will too.

Occasionally, when you are stopped, some officers are either so arrogant or thin-skinned, or just having such a bad day, that even a polite comment by you in an effort to talk your way out of a ticket is viewed by the officer and reported to the prosecutor and judge as "giving the officer a hard time". Your comments are what he writes down and remembers when you get to court. For example, I recently represented a young man on a reckless driving charge; reckless by speeding eighty-one MPH in a fifty-five MPH zone. Speeding over eighty MPH is reckless driving in Virginia, regardless of the posted speed limit. As I and most lawyers I know always do when trying to negotiate a reduced charge in such cases, I asked the State Trooper if my client gave him a hard time on the street at the stop scene. The officer replied "Yes". I then asked him what was said or done by my client, and the trooper's reply was that my client said to him that he was only keeping pace with a group of cars in which my client was the last in the group and therefore the easiest for the trooper to stop. That's a "hard time"? Most officers I knew when I was a prosecutor didn't even consider being called an S.O.B. half a dozen times or so in a twelve hour shift, a hard time. They regarded that as positive recognition that they were doing their job. Times have indeed changed.

The lesson here is you can never be sure of the mood or attitude of today's officers. So once again, the less said, the better. It is almost always better to just agree to come to court by signing the ticket and be on your way. Even if you represent yourself and explain the situation to the judge, he will invariably inquire of the officer if you were a problem on the street, and if you said nothing to the officer, and he so advises the judge, it is there, from the judge, that you're more likely to get a break if you have a good driving record. If you hire a lawyer, many judges I've appeared before, on their own, will reduce such a charge to simple speeding; particularly when the roadway was an interstate highway and you were doing nothing more than going fast—no darting between and around other vehicles—and you went to the expense of hiring a lawyer, provided your record is relatively clean. Such a reduction in the charge will be helpful when it is time to renew your insurance. Once again, the less said, the better.

> *"Discretion of speech is more than eloquence."*
> **—Francis Bacon**

At no time ever verbally insult, demean, or say to the officer things like "Go find some real criminals", or "Don't you have anything better to do?" Officers always remember these comments, write them down, and advise the prosecutor or judge of what you said. Judges see these officers in court regularly, and most judges think most officers are hardworking, risk-taking public servants who the judge doesn't like to see verbally abused on the street. It is very difficult for your lawyer to repair this type of damage.

When an officer stops you for a traffic infraction, many of which don't carry jail penalties, and in Virginia, for which the officer must give you a summons provided you sign it, these infractions are complete upon the officer's observation. By the time you hear the sirens and/or see his emergency lights, the officer has all the evidence he needs. It matters little what you say; he is either going to issue a ticket, give you a written warning, or let you go after some brief discussion which is more of a lecture by the officer telling you how bad you're driving is, and that you need to fix it.

In these situations, two pieces of advice are to be remembered. First, do not refuse to sign any ticket, citation or summons. **Always sign it.** Your signature is nothing more than your written promise to appear in court. It is required if the officer is to let you go on your way. Signing is not an admission of guilt, and refusal to sign it will get you a police escort to the judicial officer, with you in handcuffs. Second, and vitally important, be alert for any continuing conversation after you sign the ticket and your license and registration are returned to you. Ordinarily at this point, you are free to drive away. If the officer continues to talk to you, it is usually along the lines of asking about the car's contents or a direct request to search the vehicle. This happens regularly to people in the age group or who appear to the officer as those who fit a police manufactured profile or who he thinks typically use drugs or alcohol. It may be a statement/question as to your destination or where you have just come from. Something as innocent as that may tempt you to converse with the officer.

Beware! What he's looking for here is something like, you are going to or coming from a park, ballgame, picnic, party, rock concert, the beach, a school function, or anything like that. To the police, these places are where alcohol and/or pot are consumed. This is your signal to say right then, "Am I free to leave?" If you don't, and then answer him, you have fallen onto a very slippery slope. The next thing he will ask is whether there are any drugs or alcohol in the car and ask for your consent to search the vehicle. You should right then tell the officer you are leaving and have nothing to say. If he prevents you from leaving, this show of authority and your submission to it is an arrest. If he says you can leave, do so immediately!

Another technique utilized by the officer is for him to say, "We need to talk to you.", suggesting that you need to answer him. You do not have to. When he says he needs to talk to you, you need to keep quiet. Never forget that the police are totally dependent on getting you to talk in order to make or complete most cases against you, other than minor traffic infractions. This dependence is the reason why they are trained to be persistent, manipulating you, tricking you, and misinforming you under the guise of appearing friendly, in order to extract from you evidence that they have no other way of obtaining. You can short circuit their effort with a simple and prompt telling them that you are not saying anything without a lawyer present. The more they talk to you, the more they are indicating that they haven't got a good case against you without your statements. Continue to ask if you are free to leave, until you get an answer. By now, having read this far, you should know what to do, depending on the answer.

People often confuse the term *Miranda* "rights" and *Miranda* "warnings". In my view warnings is the correct term. *Miranda* does not create any rights, the Constitution does that, as the opening line of the warning states; it cites the

Fifth Amendment. The *Miranda* decision is an interpretation of the Constitution and is only a police required reminder to you of those rights. That is why it's vitally important that you keep in mind when talking to an officer and he has not arrested you and therefore not recited the warnings, that your Constitutional right to silence applies. You **always** have the right to remain silent, and until your circumstances or the announcement by the police, or the conduct of the police indicates that you are under arrest, you are free to disengage from the officer at any time, to walk away without saying anything, and doing so does not furnish grounds for arresting you.

On many TV police and law and order type shows, you often hear a detective say to someone, "Tell us what you know, or we'll take you in for questioning". That is nothing more than an idle threat having no legal support. The only time you are required to go with an officer is if you are arrested. Your response to a statement like that should be that you're not going anywhere without an arrest, and to then ask if you are free to leave. Act accordingly, depending on the officer's answer. If he arrests you, your next stop will be a judicial officer; not, as on TV, an interrogation or interview room. If he doesn't do that, remind him that you have nothing to say, demand to consult a lawyer, and to be taken to the judicial officer. Those statements should cause any competent police officer or detective to do his job, stop questioning you and get you before the magistrate. If he doesn't do that, say nothing further except demand a lawyer, using the word "demand". Do not waiver or change your mind and you'll get your way, probably sooner than later. The police often give up in frustration when you show them that you are not intimidated, which lets them know that you know your rights and are not afraid of being arrested.

Many of my colleagues think that folks can't follow any advice when confronted by the police. I believe that if you keep it simple, you can. If you have enough presence of mind to be concerned that the officer will think you're guilty if you remain silent, or refuse to take any tests on the street, you have enough presence of mind to remember the simple basic right the Fifth Amendment gives you. When the officer asks about anything, after you have identified yourself or received a summons, he suspects something, and is looking for evidence of that something. He may not say what he suspects, but let me assure you, he's looking.

If he does tip you off as to what he's thinking by specifically referring in some direct or subtle way to drinking or marijuana or searching your car, that's it. Pay attention to what's happening, think for a second or two, and decide right then and there you're done talking, and so inform the officer. If you think you can talk your way out of an arrest, once the officer indicates he's looking for drugs or talks about alcohol, forget it! It's not going to happen. You're going to be arrested. Go with the flow and let him arrest you. The less you say and do, the more likely your arrest will be illegal. Even if you think that arrest is invalid or illegal, the street is not a place to debate that issue with the officer. Neither of you are equipped with the legal knowledge to settle the question, and such discussions go nowhere. Just submit to the arrest to avoid getting hurt because he has all the tools to do so. Get off the street as quickly as possible. Just go with the officer to the magistrate.

When you sound like you know what you're doing, when you assert your rights, oftentimes the officer will launch into his take or opinion on what the law is in your situation, and how wrong or misinformed you are. Ignore him when he starts to tell you the law or tells you what you're doing by not talking to him, not answering questions, and not taking tests, is not legal or permitted, or is not a good idea. The officer is the last person in the world from whom you should accept legal advice. Most of them don't know the law, and those that think they do will slant it in their favor, advise you incorrectly, or deliberately misstate it, to get you to speak, to give them the evidence they need to justify, in their minds, your arrest. Do not ask for legal advice from the officer or ask what you should do in the situation. You should know by now exactly what five things you should do: Identify yourself, ask to leave, tell him you will not take any tests, tell the officer you have nothing else to say, and then, shut up!

Another reaction the officer might have to your asserting your rights is to tell you how good his case against you is, so you might as well tell your side, as though he was capable of being an impartial judge. This is another lie. If his case was so great against you, he would not have to ask you anything. When you assert your right to silence, another response from the officer might be, "Oh, that's not how the system works". Any officer who says that to you is out of touch with reality.

The beat of desperation by the officer goes on when he, as some clients have reported to me, tells you, "The judge will appreciate your honesty". I have a long-standing acquaintance on the bench who became a judge shortly after leaving the prosecutor's office. We converse regularly about legal issues and new court decisions. One of my recent questions to him was to ask why, in his view, defendants talk to the police and give the police the evidence they need to convict the person they arrested? The judge had a quick two word answer, "They're stupid". I followed that up with another question, "Do you give them credit for their honesty at sentencing time?" Answer, "No, they're stupid". What does that tell you about police advice to be honest with them on the street? You don't have to be dishonest, just be quiet.

The officer also may use another popular lie—telling you how much trouble you're in, and if you talk it will be better for you, or for the outcome of your case. Really? Only two things get you into, and keep you in a lot of trouble, your mouth, and the words that come out of it, nothing else. Once the officer arrests you, the only thing that should come out of your mouth is to ask him to loosen the handcuffs a bit, if he applied them too tightly.

> *"Anyone who says the truth shall set You free has never been to . . . court."*
> —Mad Magazine

The right to remain silent after you identify yourself, the right to counsel before answering questions, if arrested, the right to promptly be taken to a judicial officer after arrest, the right to say no to a request to search prior to arrest, the presumption of innocence, and the requirement that the government prove your guilt without your help, is the law in every state. These rights are essentially about **evidence**; how the government gets and uses evidence against you. Talking and testing are not about law, but about **evidence**.

Just like the misplaced focus and the misplaced reliance of the public on *Miranda*, most folks mistakenly and foolishly focus on and worry about what is the law when stopped by a police officer. Even if you knew the DUI statutes of your state well enough to recite them word for word, that won't help you during a police encounter. Stopping you is not about the law; it is all about the **evidence**. What the officer sees you do behind the wheel is **evidence**. When he stops you and asks, "Have you had anything to drink tonight", he's asking for **evidence**. When he asks you to take a preliminary on-the-street breath test, he's seeking **evidence**. When you volunteer to take the field sobriety tests, you are giving the officer **evidence**. Anything they say to get you to speak or take tests of any kind is the pursuit of **evidence**. Taking the station house breath or blood test is giving **evidence**. Every word of police speak, everything he says to you, is for that purpose only. That's what the confrontation is all about; **evidence** and nothing else!

In the final analysis, it is only the evidence and how the police get it and use it that matters. The law alone does not cause your arrest. The law alone convicts no one. It is the law and the evidence together that does the damage. You don't have to know any additional law to survive a police encounter; you just need to control your mouth. You can't control the law on the street. The only thing you can and need to control there is keeping the police from obtaining evidence and proof from you by your not voluntarily serving it up to them. On the street there isn't enough time to think about the law and then quickly make good choices about it. DUI laws are too detailed and complicated for snap judgments in the time available with a police officer in your face. I have represented lawyers who got it wrong on the street! The only law that matters at these scary moments is simple, reliable, and works in every state, in every encounter; the law that you may remain silent and not give evidence. The officer is not out there to discuss the law or test your knowledge of the DUI laws. He's there to get evidence to use as proof in court against you. All the law you need to know anywhere is remain silent and don't take any tests. That's it! All you need is the courage to remain silent and tell the officer that's what you're doing right up front, with the right tone and style. Then stop talking and remain quiet.

When I was studying for the bar exam, the instructor, a law professor from a top law school gave this advice: "Forget everything you learned in law school, everything but what I tell you, and you will pass the exam." He was right and my advice is the same. Forget everything you know or think you need to know about the law when stopped by the police except the law that you can be silent and not take any tests. You will not only survive the encounter, you should win in any state in which you may be.

While the states' DUI laws change regularly and the punishment upon conviction is ratcheted up, the rights to silence and to not test remain constant. Speaking, giving evidence, and taking tests are voluntary, not mandatory, virtually everywhere. That's all the law you need to know in those stressful moments. It's really that simple! Don't think "law", think "evidence". Remember that single word— **evidence**—and you will be okay when and where it counts, in court.

Media created and police implemented deception has caused the formation of bad habits, when it comes to police encounters. Talking, taking tests, cooperating, consenting to searches, and fearing arrest are self-destructive bad habits. Saying no to authority figures, no to talking, no to testing, no to search requests must become your new habits if you are to have any chance to avoid a conviction. Volunteer your identity and nothing else—no evidence. That's all you have to do—stop giving evidence against yourself.

SUMMATION

"*On every question of construction (let us) carry ourselves back to the time when the Constitution was adopted . . . and instead of trying what meaning may be squeezed out of the text or invented against it, conform to the probable one in which it was passed.*"

—Thomas Jefferson

"*. . . there are absolutes in our Bill of Rights and . . . they were put there on purpose by men who knew what words meant and meant their protections to be absolute.*"

—U.S. Supreme Court Justice **Hugo L. Black**

> *"Today . . . there can be no doubt that the Fifth Amendment privilege is available outside of criminal court proceedings and serves to protect persons in all settings in which their freedom of action is curtailed in any significant way from being compelled to incriminate themselves."*
> —**Chief Justice Earl Warren**, Miranda v Arizona

The decade of the 1960s witnessed great strides made for the Constitutional rights of individuals in the criminal law process. Those accomplishments had as a basic feature the concept of the interposition of a neutral independent judicial officer between the government's agents, the police, and the individual when it came to arresting and searching.

Even before that decade ended however, those rights and that notion of a neutral detached judicial officer interposed between the police and the individual began to erode by Court decisions and legislative enactments, starting with Supreme Court decisions like the seminal "stop and frisk" case of *Terry v. Ohio* in 1968. This erosion and sidestepping of these provisions of the Constitution has progressed non-stop for the past four and one half decades, with judicial and legislative exception after exception, and qualification after qualification to most of the rights of individuals contained in the Bill of Rights, as well as in the landmark United States Supreme Court decisions of the 1960's, with one notable conspicuous exception, the Fifth Amendment right to remain silent. To the present time it remains intact and unchanged.

Under the banner of "getting tough on crime" and the "wars" on crime, drugs, guns, and drunk driving, the Government declares periodically, we have seen the expansion of pre-arrest police power. This expansion has now given us police profiling, as an acceptable substitute for evidence, widespread random stopping and frisking which are based on hunches and guesswork, labeled as "good police work", the use of military style Special Weapons and Tactics (S.W.A.T.) teams for routine arrests and searches, diminishing judicial discretion in sentencing, mandatory minimum sentences and ridiculously long and excessive punishments for comparatively minor, nonviolent, victimless offenses. The result has not been pretty for the Bill of Rights and all of us who are entitled its protections. The objective legal tests for authority to arrest and search have eroded over time to less and less need for the police to give objective facts when applying to judicial officers for such approval and to more and more deference by courts to the subjective mental processes of police officers as the substitute for judicial review of facts as authority to arrest, search, and question. This erosion, combined with the virtual disappearance of the exercise of the right to silence in a smokescreen of pre-arrest, pre-*Miranda* deception, has brought about an end result for these rights that has been, and is, ugly indeed!

One such consequence has been the largest prison population in the world here in the United States, and high rates of recidivism due to the way that we crush people with their criminal history. This is followed by a "ball and chain" post-release supervision bureaucracy, effectively blocking their productive re-entry into society upon their release from custody. This is undoubtedly a contributing cause of what is keeping our young adult ex-offenders in the perpetual revolving door of unemployment, being idle on the street, being noticed there and profiled by the police, stopped and frisked, interrogated, arrested, convicted, and returned to prison. All of this has resulted in much widespread unhappiness with and about the criminal law process because court decisions have shifted the role of determining the objective facts from independent judicial officers to police officers on the street. The police have been allowed to become judges of the evidence, in effect, as Supreme Court Justice Robert Jackson noted, while engaged in the ". . . often competitive enterprise of ferreting out crime". The umpire is now the police, not neutral judicial officers.

This is not surprising or new. There has been constant tension and conflict between government power and individual rights since the Constitution was adopted. The Fifth Amendment right to remain silent, however, is the one Constitutional right that has changed the least, if at all, in 226 years. It is the most untouched by the "get tough on crime" advocates, the least questioned, debated or attacked in court, and is the most lied about, overlooked, and underused. Yet, it is the best, most enduring, non-technical, and uncomplicated defense available in the law. Perhaps this durability and this effectiveness as a defense is why, if it can't be and hasn't been diminished judicially or legislatively, it is the principle target of and has been under attack and nearly buried by the culture of deception about it, served up by the media in all its forms and by the police on the street in what is arguably a joint undertaking.

Police officers are not naturally dishonest. It's the method in which they're trained that is dishonesty based. They then dutifully use that training and status as armed authority figures to intimidate, exploit, and capitalize upon the long-running betrayal of the public by the television and motion picture industries entertaining us with misinformation pouring out of our TV's non-stop; conditioning us not to know. We have thereby been misled, have fallen victim to deceit, and to believe we can't simply say no to the police. Like lambs to the slaughter, we have made it easy for the government by opening our mouths when we don't have to.

This is what has happened and is happening every day across the country and especially to the responsible social drinker. What the U.S. Supreme Court politely called ". . . abdication through unawareness . . ." is in truth and in fact our giving up and giving in because we have been "dumbed down" by the media, and then taken advantage of by the police who think deception is fun. They are often amused by what they can and do get away with at your expense. We the people are a people deceived.

The time honored tradition of narrow, strict construction of the criminal law in favor of the accused and against the government has been yielding to broad interpretation of statutes in Court decisions leaning in favor of the police. Complaints about current policing and law enforcement practices are a direct result of this tilt away from strict construction policy and tradition, not limiting these decisions to their facts; most notably, in my view, *Terry v. Ohio*, as the justification for current "stop and frisk" policies and practice. The result has been the police too often getting the benefit of any doubt in court; not their targets, citizens and other persons.

The *Terry* case was the first major decision to allow an exception to the constitutional requirement of a warrant to search persons without first arresting them. In doing so the Supreme Court limited the scope of *Terry* very carefully to pat downs of the outer clothing for weapons, but like most police methods and tools, *Terry* has been misread and abused by law enforcement in the scope of its application. It has become the license to lie, distort, exaggerate and profile as the substitute for facts actually observed that has not gone unnoticed by the police. Its implementation has become highly intrusive upon our personal privacy, often without any factual basis.

Prosecutors and police departments having a stop and frisk policy, and the politicians supporting it, point to *Terry* as the basis for permitting such a generalized policy. The facts of *Terry* do not. The facts of that case show a specific, objective, articulable, fact based set of circumstances justifying a narrow exception to the warrant requirement, not based on subjective hunches and guesswork of zealous, overreaching police officers. This has happened, in my view, due to their apparent focusing on the vague broad non-fact specific phrase ". . . criminal activity may be afoot", unfortunately included in *Terry*, and ignoring the specific facts of that case which limit its application, because of the absence of a search warrant issued by a judicial officer as the constitution requires, ". . . upon probable caused supported by oath or affirmation . . . ".

The result has been far too many warrantless full blown searches of persons instead of much less intrusive, limited pat downs for weapons as *Terry* intended, justified on little more than the race, neighborhood, or clothing of the persons subjected to this abusive, constitutionally questionable practice, as currently carried out.

Those who advocate such a policy need to read *Terry* and its companion opinion, **Sibron v. New York** again and recognize the factual limitations of those decisions. They then need to pay more attention to Mr. Jefferson.

The same broad pro-police reading of the criminal law has happened, to a slightly lesser degree, to the *Miranda* decision. It is read by the police with a view toward to sidestepping it, instead of carrying out its spirit and purpose to maintain balance between government power and the rights of individuals when they meet the police. Thankfully, the right to silence has not suffered the same fate. Its status as absolute endures.

For all who moan and complain about the system, and say that something ought to be done, you have, and always have had, the means to repair the out-of-balance system on your own. It starts with you. To end the deception, this fraud upon us all, we only need to get back to the basics, and simply stop engaging with, talking to, and giving evidence to the police. The Fifth Amendment allows you to do so. It needs to be taught early and seriously, learned thoroughly, promoted energetically, represented truthfully and accurately in our popular culture, and used confidently and unapologetically every time you are confronted by the police. When you are informed, you won't be intimidated nor fooled by them. Individually, you can change a lot faster than the system. The right to remain silent is the gift that never stops giving once it is unwrapped by you from its cloak of deception. This absolute right is not going to change unless repealed, and that is not likely to happen in the lifetime of anyone reading this. Learn it, know it, remember it, use it, and **win**!

ABOUT THE AUTHOR

 Attorney Peter Baskin, almost daily for 48 years, has tried criminal cases in Virginia courtrooms. A graduate of the University of Hartford (B.S. 1964), and George Washington University (J.D. – 1967), his Martindale-Hubbell peer review rating is AV pre-eminent, the highest attainable for proficiency and ethical standards.

He resides in Northern Virginia with his wife, Jo Anne.

CPSIA information can be obtained
at www.ICGtesting.com
Printed in the USA
FFOW04n1218080516
23814FF